HYMNS

WE LOVE

LEADER'S GUIDE

CONTENTS

Hymns We Love Leaders Guide
Copyright © Steve and Pippa Cramer, 2023

Published by:
The Good Book Company Ltd

thegoodbook
COMPANY

thegoodbook.com | thegoodbook.co.uk
thegoodbook.com.au | thegoodbook.co.nz | thegoodbook.co.in

ISBN: 9781784988760 | Printed in India

Design by André Parker

Pippa Cramer serves on staff at Holy Trinity Claygate, Surrey, UK, with responsibility for ministry to seniors, and in 2022 was awarded an MBE in recognition of her work with older and vulnerable people. Pippa is the founder of Connections—one of the largest church-based gatherings for seniors in the UK—and she is passionate about loving and caring for older people, reducing loneliness and giving seniors the opportunity to find hope in the gospel. Pippa is a qualified occupational therapist, having specialised in the support and care of older people; she is an Ambassador for Faith in Later Life; and in 2021 she was awarded the Alphege Award for Evangelism and Witness by the Archbishop of Canterbury, Justin Welby.

Steve Cramer first came across Christians aged 14 through a local church youth group, and, ever since, his faith and love for Jesus have continued to grow. Having spent a number of years working in relief and development in Africa, Steve is now a director of two growing businesses in hospitality and social media. A regular speaker and preacher, Steve loves helping people to encounter God with both their hearts and minds. His other loves include Pippa, their two children, and their two dogs and one cat.

Welcome

Dear friend,

Thank you so much for your interest in *Hymns We Love*! This resource grew out of my work with seniors at my church in south-east England, where I have served in pastoral care and among seniors for more than ten years. We now have one of the largest church-based groups for seniors in the UK, called Connections, with over 100 attending each week.

A few years ago, we began to think about how we could be more intentional in sharing the gospel with these precious older friends. We had found that seniors were hesitant to join evangelistic courses: "What if I can't keep up?" "Will there be a test at the end?" "I went to Sunday school, so why do I need a course?" So, after a *lot* of prayer, we had the idea of using traditional hymns as a welcoming and non-threatening way to explain truths about the Christian faith, at a pace designed specifically for seniors.

Hymns are known to and enjoyed by this generation. They resonate with a lifetime of memories, even for those suffering from increasing short-term memory loss. We developed a series of talks exploring the history and lyrics of some of these favourite hymns and called it *Hymns We Love*. We have since used the material extensively in our own church, and it's proved extremely popular. It has also been tried and tested elsewhere, and was the cornerstone of the Daily Hope phone line, which received 750,000 calls during the Covid-19 pandemic. We are therefore now delighted to make it widely available for you.

Older people are the fastest-growing age demographic in Western societies. There are 12 million over-65s in the UK—some 19% of the population— and that figure is set to rise in the years ahead. In the US, older adults are expected to outnumber children by 2034. Jesus calls his people to love our neighbours, whoever they are—and the reality is that an increasing number of our neighbours are likely to be seniors.

Not only so, but many of these older people have a real need for community and connection. In recent decades, seniors have become among the most isolated in our communities. Society has changed and is changing rapidly, with many seniors feeling left behind and bewildered. Changing family structures mean that more older people than ever are living alone. And although people are living longer, sadly this also means that many are suffering more profoundly with physical illness, loneliness and isolation, dementia and mental-health struggles.

Churches have a wonderful opportunity to share God's love with this precious generation. Our vision for *Hymns We Love* is:

> *"For hundreds of thousands of older people to be given the opportunity to hear the gospel, and to discover how amazing our wonderful God is and how much he loves them."*

This will only happen as local churches and Christians take up the call to love and care for this sadly often-neglected generation. Thank you so much for your willingness to be part of that mission. The need is real, the opportunities are tremendous, and for our older friends, time may be short.

Please know that we are praying for you, and we'd love to encourage you to start with prayer too. We're excited to see what God might do for this precious older generation in answer to the prayers of his people.

Yours,

Pippa Cramer

Section 1

ABOUT

HYMNS

WE LOVE

HYMNS WE LOVE

WEEK	HYMN	KEY THEME
1	How Great Thou Art	God is the powerful, holy Creator of the universe, who longs for relationship with us.
2	Rock of Ages	Jesus was a real person, God's Son, who died to bridge the gap between us and God.
3	Amazing Grace	God's lavish grace invites us into full relationship with him, through Jesus.
4	The Lord's My Shepherd	When we follow God as our Shepherd, he promises to journey with us through life and lead us home to heaven.
5	And Can It Be?	We can have confidence in our relationship with God because it's based on what he has done and his goodness, not on what we have done and our goodness.
Christmas	Hark! The Herald Angels Sing	Jesus came into the world at Christmas to give us comfort and hope.
Easter	Thine Be the Glory	Jesus rose from death at Easter and invites us to trust him with our fears and doubts.
Any time	My Song Is Love Unknown	Jesus' death was part of God's loving plan to restore our relationship with him.

Series overview

Hymns We Love is an evangelistic series designed to introduce seniors to the good news of the gospel.

Each session explores a different aspect of the Christian faith through a familiar, well-loved hymn. At the heart of each session is a 30-minute video, which brings together music, testimony and prayer, along with a short talk which tells the story behind the hymn, and explores the meaning of the words and the Bible truths on which it is based. Week by week, the series aims to take guests on a faith journey from understanding who God is to making a personal commitment to him.

The main series comprises five sessions. There are also three additional introductory sessions, which can be used at Christmas and Easter, or as a one-off at any time of year.

The content of each video follows the same pattern:

- Welcome and introduction.

- Short interview with an older person, sharing why this session's hymn is special to them.

- The hymn, sung by our *Hymns We Love* congregation.

- A talk, reflecting on the story behind the hymn, the meaning of the words, and Bible truths to which they point.

- The hymn again, encouraging guests to reflect on the words.

- Closing prayer.

Structure of a session

How you use *Hymns We Love* will depend on your context. It can be used for larger groups in a church, church hall or community building, or in smaller groups or one to one in people's homes. It could also be adapted, shortened or simplified to use in care/retirement homes and with people with dementia.

If you already run a group for seniors at your church, you could include *Hymns We Love* as part of your regular sessions; or you could run it as a special series of events. You might choose to run your *Hymns We Love* sessions weekly or monthly—whatever you think will work best for your guests.

The structure of a session is very simple.

- Guests have time to chat over refreshments as they arrive.

- They watch the video together (or, you may choose to deliver this material "live" in person).

- There's then an opportunity to consider some discussion questions in small groups—followed by an opportunity for more refreshments!

The session is designed to be gentle and relational.

Here's how that might look for a session that begins at 10am:

- 9 am: Team arrive to set up the room, prepare refreshments and ensure the technology is working.

- 9.30 am: Team meet to pray and give information about what is happening.

- 10 am: Guests arrive. The welcome team greet and welcome guests, and give them a *Hymns We Love* Songbook. Coffee and refreshments are served. Team members are also on hand to chat to anyone who may be alone.

- 10.20 am: Leader gets people's attention and welcomes everyone, and gives an introduction to what is going to happen. It's very important at this point to ensure that all guests can see and hear adequately.

- 10.30 am: Start *Hymns We Love* video session. Each video includes an introduction, a testimony interview, watching/singing a rendition of the hymn, a short talk, listening to/singing the hymn again, and a concluding prayer.

- 11 am: Leader ends the *Hymns We Love* video and thanks everyone for coming along. He/she can suggest at this point that in small groups they discuss/chat through the suggested questions in the Songbook. Again, it is important to have at least one team member in each group to gently facilitate these discussions.

- 11.30 am: Guests leave and team clear away. Team feedback is useful at this point too.

If you prefer, you can also run *Hymns We Love* without the video episodes, by having the hymns played and sung live and talks and testimonies delivered in person, and by using the prayers and discussion questions from the Guest Songbook. The talk transcripts are included in this Leader's Guide to help you prepare and you can download accompanying slides from www.thegoodbook. co.uk/hwl.

Atmosphere of a session

Just as important as **what** is done is **how** the session feels. The overriding atmosphere of a *Hymns We Love* session should be one of **love and care**.

This **relational approach to evangelism** seems to be particularly effective with our older friends. Many do not have as many relationships as perhaps they once had, so the friendship and care you extend is especially significant. Therefore, while the content of the videos is an important part of a *Hymns We Love* session, so much of the vital work will be in person, as you love and care for your guests.

The goal is to help our older friends experience the love of God through the relationships they have with his people. Helping people feel loved and valued, ensuring that they are comfortable, building friendships, and allowing people to feel like they belong in a community are all so important. As we do these things, relationships and trust are built up over time which, in my experience, makes it easier for people to hear and receive the message of the gospel.

A number of elements are important in creating an atmosphere of love and care:

1. **Welcome.** It's vital to appreciate that coming along to any kind of new group, let alone a church group, can be really daunting. It is especially so for older people, who might live alone and not feel as confident with socialising as maybe they once were. So do everything you can to show people that they matter and that you're glad they're there, right from the moment they arrive. Many may be isolated, lonely or bereaved—so the welcome and friendship they receive as they come in is vital in helping them relax and feel at ease.

2. **Listening.** The *Hymns We Love* format allows lots of time for conversations. As you chat to guests, ask gentle questions that give people the opportunity to share—and listen to their answers! Follow up next time you meet if you can; someone remembering your recent operation, or the anniversary of your husband dying, or even your birthday means so much and demonstrates that you matter and are valued. Consider checking in with your guests between sessions, perhaps by way of a phone call. In this way, trust begins to build over time.

3. **Generosity.** From the refreshments served (if possible, for free) to the gentle support from the team, the idea is to share God's generosity, demonstrating in word *and* deed the grace we have found in Jesus—far more than we deserve.

4. **Prayer.** Prayer needs to surround and underpin every session and is absolutely vital if we want the Lord to be touching lives and bringing people to him. So I would encourage you to pray

as a team before and after each session, pray for your guests throughout the rest of the week, and do be praying in your own heart during the session itself!

Love and care is infectious—it's catching! I have found that as we seek to make those around us feel loved and cared for, valued and appreciated, they will go on to share this with others around them too, giving *Hymns We Love* a distinctly different atmosphere from other community groups that seniors might go to.

What you'll need

To run *Hymns We Love* you will need...

- a *Hymns We Love* DVD or downloadable episodes (if using).

- a Leader's Guide for each team member.

- a Guest Songbook for each guest. This contains the words for each hymn, a summary of the talk, a copy of the prayer, and discussion questions. The Songbook is intended to be a beautiful gift for guests and something to take home to help them to remember and reflect on what they've heard.

- pens to allow people to jot down notes or questions, if they'd like to.

There are also promotional materials available to help you advertise your series. You can buy invitation postcards from The Good Book Company or download them for free to print at home. We've also created a short video trailer that you can show in church services or at community groups to encourage people to come. Go to www.thegoodbook.co.uk/hwl.

Using the seasonal specials

The main *Hymns We Love* series consists of five sessions. There are also three additional stand-alone sessions: one for Christmas, one for Easter, and one that can be used at any time of year. You can use these episodes as the basis of a one-off special event, before inviting guests to join you for the full *Hymns We Love* series afterwards.

For example, you could use the Christmas session as part of a festive event, combined with Christmas crafts and mince pies, or even a Christmas lunch. Or for Easter, you could put on a spring-themed tea, decorating your space with lots of daffodils or other spring flowers. And you could use the "My Song is Love Unknown" introductory session in any number of ways: for example, as part of a special lunch, cream tea, summer event, or Remembrance/Veterans Day events.

Some people may be more likely to accept the invitation to a one-off event rather than a longer series, especially if they're unsure of what's involved—but hopefully, once they've come once and enjoyed themselves, they'll be keen to join you for more!

At the end of the video for each of these stand-alone sessions, there is an invitation to the full *Hymns We Love* series. If you do not intend to run the full *Hymns We Love* series in the near future, you can stop the video before this point.

You can download the relevant Guest Songbook pages for each of the seasonal sessions for free from The Good Book Company website, and print as many as you need (rather than providing every guest with a Songbook for a one-off event). Visit www.thegoodbook.co.uk/hwl.

Adapting *Hymns We Love* for other contexts

With a little adaptation and creativity, the *Hymns We Love* material could be used with seniors in many different settings. For example:

- **Care-home settings:** Many churches have good links with local care homes/retirement homes and have volunteers who regularly visit residents and/or run services for them. You could use *Hymns We Love* (with or without the videos) in this setting.

- **For those with memory impairment:** Often even those with advanced memory loss are able to recognise and enjoy old hymns they heard when they were younger. I've delivered a shortened version of the *Hymns We Love* material (the hymn, a short two-minute thought, and a prayer) in nursing homes for those with dementia and Alzheimer's. This takes some adaptation but is well worth it.

- **Pastoral visiting:** Your church may have a small team of volunteers or lay workers who already visit elderly and housebound people within your church's orbit; or this may be part of your or your minister's regular pattern of ministry. You could watch a *Hymns We Love* video with people in their homes when you visit, as a way to offer encouragement and open up conversations. You may want to choose a session which feels particularly relevant for their situation (for example, "The Lord's My Shepherd" during a time of bereavement or ill-health), and leave a DVD with them so that they can watch more on their own.

- **Small groups/home groups:** *Hymns We Love* could easily be enjoyed in small-group settings, if a large enough television screen is available and the home is suitably accessible

- **"Holiday at home":** A "holiday at home" is an event run over a day or several days which gives seniors the fun of a holiday/vacation, while ensuring they are still able to sleep in their own beds each night! It usually offers various activities, time to eat together, and some sort of spiritual input, often around a theme (a little like a Holiday Bible Club or Vacation Bible School, but for seniors). You could use the *Hymns We Love* sessions as the spiritual programme for an event like this (perhaps with a musical or historical theme).

- **Community groups:** The *Hymns We Love* videos could be shown in any number of community groups for seniors (e.g. friendship clubs, "Knit and Natter" groups, luncheon clubs). You could give a copy of the DVD to each of your older church members and encourage them to show it at whatever groups and clubs they are involved in, or simply to share it with their circle of friends.

Whatever points of contact you and your church have with older people, my hope and prayer is that *Hymns We Love* will provide fresh opportunities to share the love of Jesus with seniors in your community.

Section 2

GETTING READY TO RUN

BUILDING YOUR TEAM

Running *Hymns We Love* is not something you should attempt on your own! A *Hymns We Love* series is intended to be highly relational, and the bigger your team, the more time and attention you'll be able to devote to each guest who comes.

Moreover, we all need the help and encouragement of like-minded Christian friends as we seek to share Jesus with others. The Bible describes the church as like a body made of different parts: all different in their roles but all essential, and all united through Jesus: "From him the whole body, joined and held together by every supporting ligament, grows and builds itself up in love, as each part does its work" (Ephesians 4:16). You need the gifts of other people (and they need yours!) in order to make *Hymns We Love* a success.

How big a team you need to run *Hymns We Love* will vary depending on your context and how many guests you anticipate having. In an ideal world, we'd suggest having a minimum of **one team member for every four to five guests**. You'll probably need help setting up, greeting and welcoming guests as they arrive, providing and serving refreshments, chatting to guests before and after the video sessions, and clearing up afterwards. You may also want to consider having volunteers who are able to provide transport for guests to and from the session.

Approaching people

- **Prayer:** If you're starting from scratch with building a team, then the challenges can feel insurmountable! So start by praying. Bring your needs before God and ask him to provide who you need; pray that he would guide you to the people he is calling to serve in this way.

- **Identify the right people:** This isn't just about getting enough pairs of hands to do what's needed; it's about building a team of volunteers who will share your heart for reaching older people and are keen to invest in the mission of *Hymns We Love*. Develop a list of gospel-hearted people (of all ages) with different skills and giftings (listening, practical, technological, first-aid trained, and so on). Remember that nobody needs to be the finished article before they get involved—hopefully every team member will learn and grow as you serve together. If you don't know who to ask, do seek the advice of others. It may be wise to consult your church leaders too.

- **Make personal invitations:** A personal invitation is SO much better than a general plea for volunteers in the church notice sheet. In the nine months before I started up Connections, the weekly group for seniors at our church, I contacted one or two people a week and arranged to have a coffee with them. I shared the vision behind what I was seeking to do, asked them what they thought, noted down ideas and invited them to consider being part of the team. I also intentionally encouraged each person about what made them particularly special. Building people up, no matter who they are, is so important and shows them that they have something valuable to contribute.

- **Belonging before you believe:** At our group, Connections, we do have some volunteers who would not yet call themselves Christians, but who are keen to be part of something that offers companionship to older people in the community. That said, there are definitely some roles that wouldn't be appropriate for a non-Christian, and it's important that the culture of the team as a whole is distinctly gospel-shaped in flavour. But being part of the team is a great way for people who are not yet Christians to spend time with believers and be exposed to more of the gospel message. After all, we as humans enjoy being part of things, and kindness and care are catching—and this is the same for our team as well as our guests.

Training people

- **Pull the team together:** Invite your team to a team meeting to get them all together, thank them for being part of the team, and tell them again about the vision for running *Hymns We Love*. Go through practical issues, chat about who will be doing what, and, of course, pray!

- **Show the training videos:** We've created two short training videos on the "Why?" and "How?" of *Hymns We Love*, along with a range of supporting material, which you can use as the basis of one, two or more team training sessions (see page 31 of this Leader's Guide). The material is designed to be used flexibly so that you can use whichever elements you think will suit your team best. Alternatively, you could send the videos to your team members for them to watch at home.

- **Consider practical training:** Ask whether any of your team members need specific training and support for the role they're being asked to do—something that seems straightforward to you (like using a tea urn, for example) may not be so to someone who has never done it before! Training is an important part of helping team members feel confident and supported, and able to enjoy serving.

- **Provide safeguarding training as needed:** It's possible that some of your guests at *Hymns We Love* will be classed as vulnerable adults, and it's therefore important to take particular steps to safeguard them from harm. Check your church's safeguarding policy to see what training volunteers should be given if working with vulnerable adults. Speak to your church's safeguarding lead for more help.

Appreciating people

Having a happy, motivated, and appreciated team is central to *any* area of ministry being a success. If your *Hymns We Love* team feel known, valued and appreciated, this in turn will help them to get to know, value and appreciate your guests.

When we think of teams we've been part of in the past that have **not** worked well, we can probably work out why—perhaps we as team members were never consulted, or felt our opinions meant very little, and perhaps we felt demoralised and unappreciated. In contrast, in teams we've been part of that **have** worked well, we were probably thanked and appreciated for our contributions and help, our opinions were sought and we were well supported, and this in turn may well have helped us feel motivated, valued and more likely to turn up and take part.

As your *Hymns We Love* series gets under way, make a point of encouraging and thanking your team; you can do this verbally, by text and email, and by singing their praises in front of others. Try to notice specific things they've done well and tell them how much you appreciated it. Remind people regularly that they are needed and valued.

PREPARING PRACTICALLY

This section has primarily been written to help those running *Hymns We Love* with a larger group, but some of it may be helpful in other contexts too.

Venue and time

You can run *Hymns We Love* in a church, a church hall, a community centre, care home/retirement home or someone's sitting room as part of a small group—anywhere where there is a large enough screen for people to watch the videos easily.

Do think about how you can make your venue accessible and comfortable for your guests:

- Is the venue wheelchair accessible? Are there accessible toilets?

- Is there a hearing-aid loop for those who are hard of hearing?

- Are the chairs comfortable and easy to get on and off—not too low or too high?

- Is the room warm/cool enough? If it's a bit draughty, do consider providing blankets. Or if it's a warm day, have jugs of water and glasses available too.

If you already run a group for seniors, consider using this familiar venue for running *Hymns We Love*. The "familiar" is always good, and guests will not feel too daunted about coming along.

You'll also need to decide *when* to run *Hymns We Love*. In our experience, the morning is often better than the afternoon—we all tend to be more awake in the mornings! A typical session could run from 10 am until 11:30 am, giving people time to get home for lunch. But you should choose whatever you think will work best for your guests. You'll find a breakdown of the suggested timings for a session on pages 12-13.

Set-up

Think about how you will set up your space in order to make your guests comfortable and facilitate good conversations.

- **Seating:** For a larger group, we've found that having small coffee tables for people to sit around, in smaller groups of about 4 to 6 people, works well. We have tended to arrange these little groups in semicircles facing the front so that everyone can see the screen or the speaker easily. Have at least one of your helpers sitting with each little group to help facilitate conversations, especially during the discussion time after the video or talk.

- **Welcome table:** It's a good idea to have a welcome table near the entrance where guest's names and contact details can be recorded. Giving out name labels can be really helpful for everyone too. These can be as simple as sticky labels—but use a thick felt-tip pen to write the names, which will help guests with poor eyesight.

- **Decorations:** Think about the aesthetics of the room. Ensuring that everything looks lovely all helps guests to feel welcomed and valued. For example, you could consider using pretty white tablecloths on the tables, with small vases of flowers. A little decoration goes a long way in making it feel more of an occasion.

- **Refreshments:** This is **very** important. What we serve, and how we serve it, is an expression of hospitality. It demonstrates that we value and appreciate our guests. If you're going to serve coffee and tea, then try to make sure these are good quality, if possible. You may also find that using cups and saucers, rather than mugs, is appreciated. We find homemade cakes go down a treat too, but chocolate biscuits are popular as well! Or consider other refreshments that would be more culturally appropriate for your group. Have helpers on hand to serve the refreshments and help carry cups and saucers, and plates if necessary.

Advertising and inviting

Plan how you will advertise your *Hymns We Love* series and encourage people to come. The hope is for as many people as possible to come along and hear about God's love for them!

In our experience, personal invitations work best—that is, you and your team members personally asking people you know and offering to come with them. Perhaps the most obvious people to start with are those already known to you, perhaps in your church congregation or group. You can consider inviting friends, older relatives, neighbours… And of course, encourage guests to bring a friend and invite others! Do pray about this, and ask the Lord to bring to mind those who might be particularly lonely, bereaved, struggling and in need of hearing the good news of Jesus. You could drop it into a conversation and talk about what you're doing.

Also consider how you can make *Hymns We Love* known at community groups; ask if you can go in person to talk about *Hymns We Love*, rather than just passing on information.

Inviting someone to come along with you (rather than expecting them to turn up by themselves) is also tremendously helpful.

On our website you'll also find:

- invitation cards to buy or download.

- printable posters.

- a guest-friendly video trailer, which you could show in church services or at community groups.

FOLLOW-UP

Follow-up is essential! Think about how each of your guests can continue their faith journey once *Hymns We Love* has come to an end. It's likely that you'll have people at various stages: some may be uninterested in the spiritual side but will have enjoyed the social experience; others may be warmer to Christian things but not yet ready to make a commitment; and still others, we pray, will have put their trust in Jesus for the very first time. In each case, it's important to give people the opportunity to maintain the relationships they've built and to explore more of the gospel, if they wish.

If your church already runs a regular group for seniors, then an invitation to this group would be an obvious place to start. If *Hymns We Love* is a totally new venture for you, then consider arranging more gatherings involving the same team and the same atmosphere of welcome, hospitality, love and care.

For example, at my church we run a weekly group called "Connections". Just as with a *Hymns We Love* session, there is a warm welcome as people arrive, coffee and cakes are served, and team members are on hand to engage guests in conversation. The church is set up with different activities, designed to prompt conversations (for example, special-interest tables, mini hand massages, seated exercises, carpet boules, craft tables), and we have a "Thought for the day", which brings in a Christian element.

If you're not in a position to set up a group, you can continue your relationships with your guests more informally through phone calls and visits.

It's also a great idea to invite your guests to church. You could put on a special *Hymns We Love* service which includes all the hymns from the series, perhaps interspersed with short reflections on their themes. If done as part of your Sunday service, this would be a wonderful way to introduce your guests to church (and your church to *Hymns We Love*!)—or you could hold it at another time if that's not possible.

If someone has become a Christian through *Hymns We Love*, then it's particularly important that you help them to become part of your church family. Do remember that coming to church for the first time may well be daunting—so offer for someone they know to pick them up and come with them. Consider too whether there are any physical barriers that may make coming to church difficult and what can be done to overcome these.

Section 3

TEAM-TRAINING MATERIAL

HYMNS

WE LOVE

TEAM TRAINING

Training is vital in helping your team understand what *Hymns We Love* is all about and preparing you all to work together effectively. How you train your volunteers will depend on the size of your team, how well they know each other, whether you've done similar work with older people before, your church's "training culture", your team's availability and how exactly you plan to use *Hymns We Love* in your setting.

On pages 32-35 you'll find a menu of different training activities, which you can pick and choose from to build the training session(s) that will best suit your team. It is not anticipated that you will use them all—instead, focus on what your team needs and what is possible in the time you have available.

At the very least, I'd suggest watching the two training videos on the "Why?" and "How?" of *Hymns We Love*, and making time to pray together. These are available as digital downloads or on the *Hymns We Love* DVD.

For a more thorough training pathway, you could combine the training videos with other elements (such as the starter questions, discussion questions, Bible study, or brainstorming activity) as the basis of two training sessions on separate occasions, or perhaps as part of a team-building/training morning.

It's generally good to involve your team in planning decisions too, rather than simply "downloading" information to them. This way, you'll benefit from their ideas and passions, be better placed to understand and use their skills, and enable them to feel that they are really part of the team (not "just" the "tea lady" or the driver). You might also want to do a *Hymns We Love* session (or even the whole series) with your team before you run it for guests. Again, feel free to use the training resources flexibly to suit your setting and team.

Training ideas menu

Chat: Starter discussion option 1 (5-10 minutes)

Aim: To help people get to know each other and to get a sense of peoples' hopes, concerns and expectations as you begin this journey together

Go round the group and share: How are you feeling about being part of *Hymns We Love*? What are you hoping to get out of it?

Chat: Starter discussion option 2 (5-10 minutes)

Aim: To get to know each other and remind ourselves of how precious this older generation is

Go round the group and share: Tell us about an older person who has had a big impact on your life (and perhaps your faith)? What made them so special?

Watch: Training video 1: "Why run *Hymns We Love*?" (15 minutes)

Aim: To help people catch the vision for reaching older people in your community

Show the training video (available as a digital download or on the *Hymns We Love* DVD). This first part describes the vision behind *Hymns We Love* and explains why reaching seniors with the gospel is important to Jesus, and therefore should be important to us.

Discuss: Training video 1 (10-15 minutes)

Aim: To reinforce the ideas shared in training video 1 and discuss their implications

After watching the training video, use the following questions to guide your discussion:

- Was there anything in the video which struck you or surprised you?

- How would you describe the vision for running *Hymns We Love*?

How will this affect the way you view older people?

- Think back to the people, events and ideas that God used to draw you to faith in Jesus. What was it that you found compelling? How could you apply that to the older people around you?

- Share two things you will take away from this session and pray about.

Bible study: Matthew 9:35-38 (15-20 minutes)

Aim: To see Jesus' heart for the lost from Scripture

Read the Bible passage (Matthew 9:35-38) and use the following questions to explore it.

- How does Jesus respond to the lost and needy people around him? What does he do about it?

- You too were once a "sheep without a shepherd" (v 36)—but Jesus "had compassion" on you, sought you out with "the good news of the kingdom" (v 35) and brought you home to God. How does it make you feel to remember that Jesus did that for you? Humanly speaking, who did he use to do it?

- Think about some older people you know, who you would like to come to *Hymns We Love*. Do they seem "harassed and helpless, like sheep without a shepherd"? Why, or why not?

- How do verses 37-38 encourage you as you think about starting *Hymns We Love*? How do they urge you to pray?

- As those involved with a *Hymns We Love* series, we are workers in God's harvest field. What kind of worker would you like, with God's help, to be?

Finish your study with prayer, thanking Jesus for being your Shepherd, and asking him to fill you with compassion and send you out to the lost in your community.

Chat: Starter discussion option 3 (5-10 minutes)

Aim: To begin to put ourselves into the shoes of someone attending Hymns We Love for the first time

Go round the group and share: Talk about an occasion when you joined a church or community group for the very first time. What made it a good or bad experience?

Watch: Training video 2: "How to run *Hymns We Love*" (15 minutes)

Aim: To understand what a Hymns We Love session looks like and how to make it a great experience for each of your guests

Show training video 2 (available as a digital download or on the *Hymns We Love* DVD). This second part talks about how to create an atmosphere of love and care at a *Hymns We Love* session, as well as various practical considerations that need to be planned.

Discuss: Training video 2 (10-15 minutes)

Aim: To reinforce the ideas shared in training video 2 and discuss their implications

After watching the training video, use the following questions to guide your discussion:

- What struck you most about how to run *Hymns We Love* sessions? How do you feel about the emphasis on relational evangelism as a way to reach older people?

- Which aspect(s) of running *Hymns We Love* do you think you would like to be involved in?

- Can you anticipate any practical challenges with running *Hymns We Love* in your specific setting? How could these be overcome?

- Can you think of any older people that you would like to invite?

Are there any other people you think it would be good to invite?

Brainstorm: Practical plans (15 minutes)

Aim: To gather people's ideas and allow them to be involved in the planning process

Start by sharing any specific practical plans already in place for your *Hymns We Love* sessions. Then, using a whiteboard or a large piece of paper, brainstorm ideas for how you could make your *Hymns We Love* sessions a really positive experience for guests in your context. Think about the areas mentioned in the video:

- Atmosphere (love and care)

- Venue

- Set-up (including refreshments)

- Advertising and inviting people

Decide which ideas you are going to action, and assign them to a member of the team to make them happen.

Pray: Prayer time (10 minutes)

Aim: To commit your plans to God in prayer

Spend time in prayer for *Hymns We Love*, using the following prompts to guide you.

- Thank God for each member of your team and the different gifts and skills he has given each of you.

- Pray for people you plan to invite to *Hymns We Love*; and ask God to bring others to mind too.

- Ask God to help you to love and care for your guests, and commit all your practical plans to God's care.

- Pray that as you and others like you reach out to seniors in your communities, "hundreds of thousands of older people will be given the opportunity to hear the gospel and to discover how much our wonderful God loves them".

Section 4

SESSION NOTES AND
TALK SCRIPTS

HYMNS
WE LOVE

1. HOW GREAT THOU ART

O Lord, my God, when I in awesome wonder
Consider all the works Thy hands hath made,
I see the stars, I hear the mighty thunder,
Thy power throughout the universe displayed:

Then sings my soul, my Saviour God, to Thee,
How great Thou art, how great Thou art!
Then sings my soul, my Saviour God, to Thee,
How great Thou art, how great Thou art!

When through the woods and forest glades I wander
And hear the birds sing sweetly in the trees;
When I look down from lofty mountain grandeur,
And hear the brook, and feel the gentle breeze:

Then sings my soul...

And when I think that God, His Son not sparing,
Sent Him to die, I scarce can take it in:
That on the cross, my burden gladly bearing,
He bled and died to take away my sin.

Then sings my soul...

When Christ shall come, with shout of acclamation,
And take me home, what joy shall fill my heart!
Then I shall bow in humble adoration
And there proclaim, my God, how great Thou art!

Then sings my soul...

Carl Boberg, translated from the Swedish by Stuart K. Hine.
© 1949 and 1953 by the Stuart Hine Trust CIO.

About this hymn

- It was written in 1885 by Carl Boberg—a Swedish sailor-turned-hymn writer—under the title "O Store Gud".

- Boberg published more than 60 poems, hymns and songs, but this one is easily his most famous.

- It was translated into the English version we know and love today by Stuart K. Hine in 1948.

Exploring the Christian faith

The Bible says that the wonderful world around us points us to God, the Creator:

- He is a God who is powerful and holy, set apart from us, and…

- He is a God who loves his creation, loves us and wants a relationship with us.

"For my thoughts are not your thoughts, neither are your ways my ways," declares the LORD. "As the heavens are higher than the earth, so are my ways higher than your ways and my thoughts than your thoughts."

ISAIAH 55:8-9

Questions to consider

- How do you feel when you look at the natural world around you?

- Are there particular aspects of creation that you enjoy or marvel at?

- Why did God create all of this, and create us, do you think?

- Has the hymn made you think differently about God's holiness or his love?

Prayer

Dear Lord,

Thank you that you are a powerful, great God, who created the entire universe and trillions of stars with just the power of your word.

Thank you also that you love the beauty and detail of life, taking joy in peaceful forest glades and exquisite bird song as well as in the splendour of the lofty mountains.

Most of all, thank you that you love and take joy in your relationship with us, your people.

Help me to know your love, to experience your joy and to see the world around me, and people around me, as you do.

As I reflect on these wonderful hymns, please help me to take a step closer to you each day—to see you more clearly, love you more dearly and follow you more nearly.

In Jesus' name,

Amen

Script for Session 1
"How Great Thou Art"

The former US president Abraham Lincoln reportedly once said that "if you took all the people who fell asleep in church on Sunday morning and laid them out end to end… they would at least be a great deal more comfortable!"

Well, as we start this short series looking at some of our favourite hymns, I hope that, at the very least, you are sitting comfortably—and I promise I will do my best to try and help you stay awake.

Together, we are going on a short journey to explore the Christian faith through five of our favourite hymns.

And my hope and prayer is that over the coming sessions, each of us will discover something new about the God these hymns were written about.

And to kick us off today, we have this incredibly uplifting hymn, "How Great Thou Art", which revels in the wonders of creation and helps point us to a powerful, holy and creator God.

It was in 1990 that the Hubble Space Telescope was launched. It took 13 years and at least 1½ billion dollars to build, but for the first time gave humankind the opportunity to observe some of the most distant parts of the universe. It quickly helped scientists develop their understanding of the cosmos, but ironically, it was only in 1995, with most of the staff off for their Christmas holidays, that our understanding of the universe was transformed.

That Christmas, with no one around and nothing better to do, NASA's director, Robert Williams, decided to just leave the telescope pointing at a tiny, pitch black, apparently empty patch of sky no bigger than the size of a grain of sand held at arm's length.

No one was expecting to find much in this part of the sky, and so, when the team returned after Christmas, they were astonished to find this apparently empty fragment of the universe contained not one or two stars but hundreds and hundreds of galaxies, each one containing billions of stars.

That accidental discovery transformed our understanding of the scale and complexity of the universe. Astronomers are now confident that there are trillions of galaxies, each one with billions of stars, and that the universe is far bigger and more glorious than we ever could have imagined.

As Professor Jim Al-Khalili, a theoretical physicist and broadcaster, said, "It is impossible not to … be intimidated by the extraordinary depth of the cosmos".

Now, Carl Boberg, who wrote today's wonderful hymn, didn't have the benefit of a space-age telescope, but, like many of us today, he could still look up at the sky and find wonder. And in its creation, he saw the work of an incredible Creator.

Carl was born the son of a carpenter in Sweden in 1859. He started out as a sailor, and you can imagine how at night, out on the northern seas, he might have looked up at the stars and wondered just how they came to be there.

After the sea, Carl went to Bible school, and later became a member of the Swedish parliament. He published more than 60 poems, hymns, and songs, but "How Great Thou Art" is easily his most famous.

Carl saw a universe of beauty, power, and wonder, and in that recognised the fingerprints of a beautiful, powerful and wonderful God... a God so great he could create trillions of stars with, as the Bible tells us, just the power of his voice.

But Carl also saw a God who was interested in the detail: the forest glades, the birds singing sweetly in the trees, as the hymn puts it.

A God who not only knows every star but lovingly created every leaf, who is intimately involved in the beauty and detail of life and who finds joy in birdsong—just as we do.

Carl saw creation as expressing something utterly central about who God is... But here's the funny thing: if we look to the Bible, it spends very little time talking about HOW this creation happened—in fact it deals with the creation of billions of galaxies and trillions of stars with just the first ten words.

"In the beginning, God created the heavens and the earth" and then a little later adds the throwaway line: "and he also made the stars…"

Now, if you know just one thing about the Bible, you will know it's quite a long book. So, if the creation of the whole universe is covered with just a few words, what are the remaining 1,500 pages or so all about?

Well, the Bible was never meant to be a science textbook. Its emphasis is not so much on the exact HOWS of creation—but on the WHO and the WHY. Who is this creator God? And why did he make us?

And as the Bible continues, so the answers to those questions unfold. Maybe you can remember some of the Old Testament Bible stories—ones like Adam and Eve, Joseph and his dreamcoat, Moses crossing the Red Sea, or the Ten Commandments.

Well, I would suggest that when you put all of these stories together, they can be summed up as saying just two things.

Firstly, they were written to help us understand just how big, how powerful, but also how holy the God who created the stars is.

But secondly, they then reassure us that this great big, powerful God actually loves us and longs to be in relationship with us.

Let's just think about the first theme for a moment. When we look at the world around us and the skies above us, we're prompted to ask: what kind of being could make all this? If there really is a Creator God, then he must be unimaginably powerful—and therefore must be very, very different to us.

But there's a problem. The Bible tells us this difference between us and God isn't just about scale and power... it is also about goodness. God is different to us because he is good—and sadly, we are not...

It may not be popular to admit it, but if we are honest, I think we could all agree that, at times, our thoughts and actions do not live up to the standards that we set for ourselves, let alone any standards that a God might set for us. When we consider all the tragedies of this world—from relationship and family breakdown through to wars and the environmental calamity we are facing—all have at their root and cause an element of human selfishness, be that individual or collective.

And that is why the Bible tells us that God is different from us both in terms of his power and his goodness, and the term it uses to describe this difference is "holy", which literally means "set apart".

The book of Isaiah says, "For my thoughts are not your thoughts, neither are your ways my ways, declares the LORD. As the heavens are higher than the earth, so are my ways higher than your ways and my thoughts than your thoughts."

God is, and by definition has to be, holy, set apart, perfect, and perfectly good. If he wasn't those things, then he wouldn't be God!

But just how set apart is he?

Let's imagine for the moment that we have all flown off to Dubai to visit the Burj Khalifa, the tallest building in world…

And someone has set a scale from the top to bottom, so that you can rank everybody who has ever lived in terms of how good they are or how well they have lived.

Now, if you were doing that, who would you put at the top?

Maybe Mother Teresa or Nelson Mandela?

And at the bottom perhaps Hitler or Stalin.

Now with that as a range, where would you put yourself? Somewhere near the top or maybe a bit lower?

And finally, having done all that, where should God be on the scale?

I guess he must be somewhere above Mother Teresa and Nelson Mandela… maybe at cloud level or perhaps the moon?

Well, what all these stories in the Bible tell us is that he is infinitely beyond that, beyond the furthest reaches of what even the Hubble Telescope can see. He's off the scale completely!

"As the heavens are higher than the earth, so are my ways higher than your ways."

After all, no matter how wonderful Mother Teresa or Nelson Mandela may be, it would still be a bit disappointing if God was just a slightly better version of them—and I have no doubt that they would be the first to agree!

The truth is that the whole range of humanity, from the very worst to very best, doesn't even register on the scale of God's goodness.

The gap between us and him is so big, there is no way you or I, by our own efforts, can ever close it.

Now, if we stopped there, believing that was the end of the story, then that would be bad news. But there is good news because it is not the end of the story... because God never stops there.

There is a second theme to all those Bible stories: God loves us and wants to have a relationship with us, despite our near-constant ability to mess that relationship up! Those Old Testament stories of Adam and Eve, of Abraham, of Moses, of David and of the Israelites are all about God reaching out to teach them who he was and to show them just how much he loved them—always in the hope that they would love him back and would share his love with others.

And although they often didn't listen to him and time after time went wrong and lost the plot, God never gave up on them... and he never gives up on us.

Despite all their failings, God kept loving and kept longing for relationship and ended up demonstrating that perfectly through the life, death and resurrection of Jesus.

And coming back to today's hymn, we see the same link, as the words move seamlessly from the wonders of creation and a Creator God in verse 2 to the story of Jesus and the cross in verse 3.

And that is the wonderful story of God's love for you and me that we remember every Easter, and which we will explore a little more in our next session when we sing "Rock of Ages".

It's the story of a God who is powerful and holy but who has also made a way for us to know him, through Jesus. And if we truly know that, then we can't help but sing in response, "How great thou art".

But then again, maybe you're not so sure. I'm sure there'll be some people watching this who like the hymns and the history but who aren't convinced by all the God stuff and can't see how it is relevant.

Well, if that is you, we're thrilled you're here with us. You may have reached that view because you just can't quite believe in a God or because you may feel that all religions basically point to the same vague higher presence, or maybe you just think that Christians and Christianity are all a bit too strange or a bit too much hard work.

Perhaps you have been bruised by past experiences of the church. Or perhaps you've been a Christian for some time, but your faith just feels a little faded or rusty.

Well, wherever you are at—whether you'd call yourself a Christian or not—you are very welcome, and I would love it if you felt able to join us as we explore these well-loved hymns, and maybe, just create a little space to think again about the Christian God. For, as one writer put it, "Christianity is a statement which, if false, is of no importance, and, if true, of infinite importance. The one thing it cannot be is moderately important."

So, please come on a journey with me through our next four hymns and reach your own conclusion about whether there is a God who created this enormous and beautiful universe—and whether he really is worth getting to know.

2. ROCK OF AGES

Rock of Ages, cleft for me,
Let me hide myself in Thee;
Let the water and the blood,
From Thy wounded side which flowed,
Be of sin the double cure;
Cleanse me from its guilt and power.

Not the labour of my hands
Can fulfil Thy law's demands;
Could my zeal no respite know,
Could my tears for ever flow,
All for sin could not atone;
Thou must save, and Thou alone.

Nothing in my hand I bring,
Simply to Thy cross I cling;
Naked, come to Thee for dress;
Helpless, look to Thee for grace;
Foul, I to the Fountain fly;
Wash me, Saviour, or I die.

While I draw this fleeting breath,
When mine eyelids close in death,
When I soar to worlds unknown,
See Thee on Thy judgment throne,
Rock of Ages, cleft for me,
Let me hide myself in Thee.

Augustus M. Toplady

About this hymn

- It was written by Augustus Toplady while he was serving as a curate in Blagdon, Somerset, England, in 1776.

- A popular story is that he wrote the hymn on the back of a playing card while sheltering from a storm in a cave.

- However, it is more likely that he was inspired by this verse from the Bible: "Trust in the LORD for ever, for the LORD … is the Rock eternal" (Isaiah 26:4).

Exploring the Christian faith

- Jesus was a real, historical person; he lived and died 2,000 years ago in what is now modern-day Israel.

- He claimed to be the Son of God. He said he was the way to God, the truth about God, and life itself.

- The Bible tells us that Jesus chose to die on the cross to pay the price necessary to restore our relationship with God, and to show just how loved and precious each of us is to God.

Jesus answered, "I am the way and the truth and the life. No one comes to the Father except through me."

JOHN 14:6

Questions to consider

- Did you know this hymn already? If so, what did you think about it?

- Who was Jesus? What do/can we know about him?

- Why is the cross so important to Christians?

- Has today made you think about the cross in a different way?

Prayer

Dear God,

Thank you that you chose to pour out your love on me—that through the life, death, and resurrection of Jesus, you offer to pick me up, wash me clean and make me whole.

Thank you, Lord, that all of this was done by Jesus, and none of it depends on how good, or how bad, I have been. You love me regardless, and I am priceless in your eyes.

Help me now to know and accept your kind and wonderful gift of forgiveness.

In the name of Jesus, I pray.

Amen

Script for Session 2 "Rock of Ages"

If you search for "Rock of Ages" on the internet, the first thing that comes up is not the hymn we just sang but the 2012 musical comedy of the same name starring Tom Cruise. The film tells the story of two young people chasing their dreams through the bright lights of Los Angeles, and its strapline promises, "Nothin' but a good time".

In many ways, it couldn't be more different from the hymn we just sang or the man who wrote it, because I suspect that, for most of us, when we think of the hymn "Rock of Ages", the phrase "Nothin' but a good time" couldn't be further from our minds.

It's a big, weighty, serious hymn, and I can understand how it might feel a bit downbeat and depressing.

But I hope that as we dig a little deeper into it today, you will come to see that although it remains a serious hymn, it does also point to something wonderful and beautiful about just how long and high and deep and wide God's love is for you and for me.

In many ways, the hymn is not dissimilar to its writer.

Augustus Toplady was a complex individual and not easy to get to know.

On the one hand, he was gentle, humble, caring and loved by his parishioners.

But he was also a bit of a loner who became embroiled in a bitter theological dispute which for many years tainted his reputation.

Born in Farnham, England, in 1740, his father was a major in the Royal Marines, who sadly died just five months after Augustus was born.

He grew up an only child and formed a pretty solitary figure for much of his short life, dying when he was just 38.

He found faith as a teenager, was ordained as a church minister when he was just 22, and initially served as a curate in Blagdon, Somerset, close to the Cheddar Gorge.

And, if you believe the sign inscribed on a rock in nearby Burrington Combe, it was here, as Augustus sheltered from a violent storm, that the inspiration for "Rock of Ages" came to him, and he quickly scribbled the words down on the back of a playing card.

It's a wonderful and memorable story but sadly almost certainly untrue! In fact, his inspiration was probably, like Augustus himself, a little less flamboyant, coming from a verse in the book of Isaiah that says:

"Trust in the Lord for ever, for the Lord our Lord is a Rock of Ages."

If you were with us when we sang "How Great Thou Art", you may remember that we explored how God is the Creator of an amazing, vast and complex universe.

We reflected how his greatness and his goodness made him so different from us—"holy", as the Bible calls it. On the one hand, that makes him worthy of our praise.

But on the other hand, the difference in his goodness and ours creates a gap, a chasm between us, that no human can cross on their own.

But we also saw that God longs for relationship with us—he longs to bridge that chasm—and that he demonstrated this by sending his Son, Jesus, to live with us, die for us

on the cross and then rise from the tomb three days later.

And it is the cross that is at the centre of the Christian faith and is at the centre of this hymn.

But before we explore that further, let's just consider for a moment who that man on the cross was, and what we can actually know about him?

Well, the first thing is, there can be no doubt that Jesus was real.

There really was a man called Jesus who lived 2,000 years ago in what is now modern-day Israel, who was hailed as a prophet and who was executed and died on a cross under the Romans.

The evidence for this is overwhelming, not just from Christian sources but also from Jewish and Roman writers and records at the time.

So, the question we need to ask ourselves is not whether Jesus existed, but WHO Jesus really was…

If you ask most people in this country who Jesus was, they will probably say he was a good man—a moral teacher who taught about love and how to live a good life.

And they are absolutely right—to a

point—because if we look carefully at what Jesus actually said about himself, I don't think he ever intended us to conclude he was just a moral teacher.

He is someone who said, "I am the light of the world", "I am the resurrection", "I am the way and the truth and the life". Jesus wasn't claiming to point the way or to teach the truth. He was claiming to BE the way and to BE the truth and to BE life itself.

When we consider all the things Jesus said and did in the Gospels, it can only mean one thing: Jesus was claiming to be God!

The writer C.S. Lewis sums it up very clearly, if somewhat bluntly:

He wrote, "A man who was merely a man and said the sort of things Jesus said would not be a great moral teacher. He would either be a lunatic—on the level with the man who says he is a poached egg—or else he would be the Devil of Hell. You must make your choice. Either this man was, and is, the Son of God, or else a madman or something worse."

The choice is ours to make.

The other thing about Jesus is that for all his teachings and for all the quality of his life, his primary focus, and the focus of the New Testament and of Christians down the ages, has not been so much on his life but on his death and resurrection.

Have you ever considered what an odd symbol the cross is?

We wear it round our necks; it is the shape of most ancient churches; many people make the sign of it when they pray.

But if I was talking to you today wearing a guillotine or a model of an electric chair round my neck, you would think I'm rather odd... and yet we think nothing of wearing a symbol of arguably the most brutal and cruel form of execution ever invented.

So why do Christians focus so much on the cross? Why are almost one third of the Gospels—the Bible's accounts of Jesus' life—about his death?

The answer is that Christians believe it is through, and ONLY through, Jesus' death and subsequent resurrection that our relationship with God can be restored—that the chasm between us and God can be bridged.

Now that is quite a statement...

and it leads to an obvious question: WHY?

Why did it all need to be so dramatic? If God is God, why couldn't he just wave his magic wand and make us friends with him?

Well, let me tell you a story to try to explain…

Once upon a time, there were two small boys who went to school together and became the very best of friends.

However, as they grew up, their lives went in very different directions.

One did well, went to university, studied law and became a successful lawyer and senior judge. But the other fell on hard times, got in with a bad crowd and turned to a life of petty crime.

The years went by, and there came a point where he was arrested and sent for trial before a senior judge. That judge turned out to be his old school friend, who recognised him and realised he faced a dilemma.

As a judge, he couldn't just ignore what his friend had done—if he ignored the law, then the law would have no value, and it wouldn't be fair.

But equally he and his friend had a long history. He could see how he had suffered.

And though his friend was undeniably guilty, he still loved him.

So, as a judge, he found his friend guilty and handed down the correct full sentence of a large fine. That was justice, and he had to do that to be true to his own standards and to the law.

But he was also a friend who loved the man. So he took off his robes, came down to the dock and wrote out a cheque. He then gave it to his friend, saying he would pay the penalty in full and his friend could now walk free.

To paraphrase St Anselm, a 12th-century Archbishop of Canterbury:

Only man SHOULD pay for his sins, since it was he who was in default.

Only God COULD make this payment, since it was he who demanded it.

It is at the cross where Christianity is shown to be different to every other religion. It confronts straight on the seriousness of sin and its impact on our relationship with a holy God, with each other and with this world.

But it then also makes clear that we can do nothing to solve that problem by ourselves. The only one who can resolve the problem is God himself.

And that is what Augustus Toplady makes so clear in this wonderful hymn:

"Not the labour of my hands can fulfil Thy law's demands."

No matter how hard we try, we can never meet God's standards. We can't ever be good enough or do enough. As we saw when we looked at "How Great Thou Art", that gap between us and God is just too big.

"Could my zeal no respite know, could my tears forever flow…"

Also it doesn't matter how earnest we are, how good our intentions are or how sorry we are.

"All for sin could not atone."

Nothing we do can make us good enough to close that gap between us and God. And that is why…

"Thou must save, and Thou alone."

In the end, everything has to come from God. Only God can rescue us.

And therefore, Augustus Toplady concludes that we are utterly helpless before God:

"Nothing in my hand I bring; simply to your cross I cling;

"Naked, come to you for dress, helpless look to you for grace;

"Foul, I to the Fountain fly; wash me, Saviour, or I die."

Phew!

Does this all sound somewhat downbeat? We certainly seem to have come quite a long way away from that Tom Cruise promise of "Nothin' but a good time!"

But whilst I appreciate that what we are discussing is serious, I don't think it need be depressing… and I don't think this is what Augustus Toplady intended.

You see, whilst at the cross I cannot escape my emptiness before God's holiness and majesty, NEITHER can I escape that God loved me and YOU so much that he paid the ultimate price to bring us back into relationship with him.

Probably the most famous verse in the Bible puts it this way: "For God so loved the world that he gave his one and only Son, that whoever believes in him shall not perish but have eternal life".

On one level, the cross shows us to be HELPLESS, naked and lost, but alongside this, Jesus' death also reveals that you and I are, in fact, utterly PRICELESS because God did, and gave, everything to close that gap—to restore that relationship so that we could enjoy a life for ever with him rather than endure one for ever without him.

On the cross, Jesus—God himself—paid the highest price possible to redeem us, to rescue us, to forgive us—to pay that debt that we owed.

And that is the unimaginable value that God places on you and me.

And that really is something wonderful!

You see, if you and I were responsible for restoring our relationship with God, we could never really be sure if we were good enough, if we had done enough, if we were safe.

I can't even keep to the speed limit. If I had to rely on myself to be good enough for God, I would be on pretty shaky ground!!

Instead, God's rescue plan for us was started and has been completely finished by Jesus. It is rock solid—God is our Rock of Ages—all we need to do is say thank you and accept this most wonderful gift that he offers.

But of course, Jesus' death on the cross is not the end of the story—it doesn't end on Good Friday, when Jesus is placed in the tomb.

Because after Good Friday comes Easter Sunday.

After the cross comes the resurrection.

And after payment of the penalty comes the freedom—of a life lived to the full.

And that is what we will explore next time when we sing the hymn "Amazing Grace".

But for now, let's sing Rock of Ages again and remember that even though we come to him with nothing, God has given everything to have a relationship with me and with you.

3. AMAZING GRACE

Amazing grace! How sweet the sound,
That saved a wretch like me!
I once was lost but now am found,
Was blind but now I see.

'Twas grace that taught my heart to fear,
And grace my fears relieved;
How precious did that grace appear
The hour I first believed!

Through many dangers, toils and snares
I have already come;
'Tis grace has brought me safe thus far,
And grace will lead me home.

The Lord hath promised good to me;
His word my hope secures;
He will my shield and portion be
As long as life endures.

When we've been there ten thousand years,
Bright shining as the sun,
We've no less days to sing God's praise
Than when we first begun.

John Newton

About this hymn

- "Amazing Grace" was written by John Newton in 1772 for a prayer service at his church in Olney, Buckinghamshire, England.

- As a younger man, he had worked on slave ships transporting enslaved people from Africa to the Caribbean.

- A near-death experience caused him to throw himself on God's grace—and this proved to be a real turning point.

- Later in life, he joined with others in campaigning for the Abolition of the Slave Trade Act (1807).

Exploring the Christian faith

- God's grace is extravagant, undeserved and... utterly wonderful.

- It goes much further and deeper than "just" forgiveness.

- It restores us to a full and close relationship with God.

"While [the son] was still a long way off, his father saw him and was filled with compassion for him; he ran to his son, threw his arms round him and kissed him … 'Let's have a feast and celebrate. For this son of mine was dead and is alive again; he was lost and is found.'"

LUKE 15:20, 23-24

Questions to consider

- What does the word "grace" mean to you?

- Can you identify with the son in Jesus' parable at all? In what way?

- What do you think about the way in which the father reacted? Is that what you expected? Do you think God could ever react to you in the same way?

- What do you think of the idea that we can have a relationship with God as our Father? What might it look like?

Prayer

Dear Lord,

Thank you that no matter how far I wander away from you, you will always be there waiting, like the father in the story of the prodigal son, ready to run towards me with your arms open wide, to pick me up, hug me and welcome me back to be at your side.

Thank you that the life of John Newton shows how this is true even for those of us who feel so undeserving.

Lord, maybe for the first or for the hundredth time, I turn to you now and say I am sorry for all that I have done wrong. Please forgive me, wash me clean and take me back into your arms.

I ask this in the name of Jesus and in confidence that you hear me and love me.

Amen

Script for Session 3 "Amazing Grace"

According to Jerry Bailey, a top executive in the music industry, *Amazing Grace* "may be the most-recorded song on the planet".

It has been recorded nearly 7,000 times by a whole range of people from Aretha Franklin to Elvis Presley.

From the bagpipes of the Royal Scots Dragoon Guards…

… to an alternative rock band called the Lemonheads.

So, what is it about this hymn, written 250 years ago by a rural English clergyman called John Newton, that still seems so relevant to people even today?

Maybe it's because it speaks so simply and eloquently about a life turned around and a hope still to come.

If you were with us when we sang "Rock of Ages", you may remember we explored why Jesus chose to die on a cross and how that created a way back for us to have a relationship with God. But the wonderful thing is, that story didn't end on Good Friday with Jesus' death but continued on to Easter Sunday and his resurrection.

And it shows us that Jesus was not just saving us FROM something but was also saving us FOR something—for a wonderful new life with him, free from guilt and full of what Christians call "grace".

And perhaps the best way to explore what grace means is to have a look at one of best-known stories that Jesus told—the parable of the prodigal son.

It's the story of a rich man who has two sons, and one day the younger one comes to his father and asks for all of his inheritance, even though his father is still fit and well! Incredibly, his father gives it to him, but instead of using the money sensibly, the son runs off and squanders the lot on wild living.

Once the money runs out, the son goes through a terrible time, ending up completely destitute and starving, living with pigs.

It is here, when he has reached rock bottom, that he finally comes to his senses and realises that even his father's servants are better off than him, and—although he has blown his chance to be treated as a son—

perhaps he could go back to work for his father as a servant. Then at least he would be fed and have a place to sleep.

So, he heads off home. And this is how Jesus describes what happens next:

"When he was still a long way off, his father saw him. His heart pounding, he ran out, embraced him, and kissed him. The son started his speech: 'Father, I've sinned against God, I've sinned before you; I don't deserve to be called your son ever again.'

"But the father wasn't listening. He was calling to the servants, 'Quick. Bring a clean set of clothes and dress him. Put the family ring on his finger and sandals on his feet. Then get the best heifer and roast it. We're going to feast! We're going to have a wonderful time! My son is here—given up for dead and now alive! Given up for lost and now found!' And they began to have a wonderful time."

You see, the father wasn't in the slightest bit interested in JUST rescuing his son from the mess he was in—he wanted FAR MORE. He loved his son so much that he wanted to totally restore him to the place he was before it all went wrong.

That's why he put the family ring of authority on his finger... and that's why he had such a huge party.

And THAT is what grace is.

It is free.

It is extravagant.

And it is very costly to the giver.

Like the father in the story, God doesn't want to just rescue us from our mess; he wants to share his love, his forgiveness—all that he is—with us, to restore us to our place as his children, with all that that entails.

And John Newton, who wrote today's hymn, really understood what it meant to be taken on that journey by God, as I think it fair to say that he tested the story of the prodigal son to its extreme.

The son of a Merchant Navy captain, John's mother died when he was seven, and, perhaps understandably, he became very unruly. After being sacked from his first job, he was press-ganged into the Navy. He deserted, was caught, flogged and eventually began working on the slave ships transporting enslaved people from Africa to the Caribbean.

From here, his behaviour continued

to decline: he beat people, probably raped women and behaved utterly appallingly. His actions left him unemployable, and he ended up reduced to rags, put in chains and begging for food—just like the son in our parable.

He was eventually rescued and was heading back to England by ship when he encountered a massive storm. The ship he was travelling on was badly damaged and was close to sinking.

As Newton struggled at the wheel of the ship, expecting to die, his mind turned to his childhood and the stories of God he'd heard from his mother, and for the first time in his life, he wondered if those stories might actually be true.

Well, the ship survived the night and incredibly a further four weeks at sea, eventually drifting into Ireland with all supplies gone. Newton was convinced that it was only God who had saved him, and there and then vowed to follow God for the rest of his life.

But things were not that straightforward. Though he tried hard to become a better person, to read his Bible and even stop swearing,

he continued to work in the slave trade and on his very next trip to Sierra Leone, quickly fell back into the absolute worst of all his old ways, seemingly powerless to stop himself.

He then caught a terrible fever, and as he lay sick, despair utterly overwhelmed him. He realised he was even worse than the prodigal son because he had had his chance to return and had thrown it away—he had effectively rejected God twice, so surely there was no way back for him now.

He ended up crawling to a remote corner of the island he was staying on and there, in his own words, "cast himself before the Lord, who should do with him as he pleased".

He had reached such a low that he no longer cared what happened to him—all he could do was throw himself on God's mercy without even much hope of an answer.

There was no sudden flash of light, but afterwards he was always clear that this was the point where everything changed. He recovered his strength, returned to England, got married and began to rebuild his life.

Fifteen years later, he became an

Anglican minister and eventually became vicar of Olney in Buckinghamshire, where he set up a regular Thursday evening prayer service. It was his habit to write a weekly hymn for this, and so it was in 1772, no doubt reflecting on the journey of his life, that he wrote "Amazing Grace".

To finish his story, he had by this point realised the evils of the slave trade, joining with William Wilberforce and others to campaign for end of slavery. And then finally, just nine months before he died in 1807, the Abolition of the Slave Trade Act was passed, helped in no small part by the life and work of John Newton.

You can therefore see that when he wrote "Amazing grace! How sweet the sound that saved a wretch like me!" he really knew what he was talking about. He knew what God had rescued him FROM and could also see what God had rescued him FOR.

He could see that it was God's grace—God's endless love and forgiveness—that kept him safe "through many dangers, toils and snares".

But he could also see that God had gone so much further than just rescuing him—so much further than only forgiving him; he had completely restored him to the place he was always meant to be: close to God, in full and loving relationship. And that is amazing grace in action.

And I'd like to end with one more example of grace in action, and that is from the story of *Les Misérables*.

At its centre is one man, Jean Valjean, who has just been released from 19 years in prison for stealing a loaf of bread to feed his starving sister. He is bitter and angry with the world.

Rejected by everyone he comes across, he is finally offered rest and food at the house of a kind bishop.

However, instead of being grateful, he returns the favour by stealing much of the bishop's silver! But he is then caught by soldiers and dragged back to the bishop's house to face justice.

Expecting to be thrown back in prison, what happens next amazes him and turns his life around.

Instead of condemning him, the bishop throws open his arms and explains to the soldiers how delighted he is to see Valjean again because Valjean had clearly forgotten to take all of the silver he had been given by the bishop! In fact, he had left behind the most valuable pieces of all—two silver candlesticks—and now he had a chance to collect them!

The soldiers then leave, and the bishop, handing over the candlesticks to Valjean, says in a low voice:

"Jean Valjean, my brother, you no longer belong to what is evil but to what is good. I have bought your soul to save it… And I give it to God."

Now when Valjean was dragged back to the house, the bishop had three choices.

He was entitled to seek justice—to get back his stolen silver and demand that Valjean be charged with theft.

Alternatively, he could have shown mercy—forgiven Valjean and released him to go on his way, but still take back the stolen silver. That would have been more than generous.

But he actually went much further than that; he showed excessive mercy—true grace. He restores Valjean's life, returning him to a position far better than even before he first went to jail.

That is exactly what John Newton experienced in his life and is how the father responded in the story of the prodigal son.

And that level of generosity is what God offers to you and me. Just like the characters in our three stories, it's more than we could have expected, more than we rightfully could have asked for and certainly more than we deserve.

And just like the characters in our three stories, our lives can be turned around by accepting God's generous gift of grace.

As we saw when we sang "Rock of Ages", justice is served through Jesus' death on the cross, and mercy is shown by God's forgiveness of all that we have done wrong.

But just like the father in the story of the prodigal son, God doesn't stop there. He is not just interested in rescuing us from our own mess—he wants so much more. He wants to restore each one of us to a place right next to HIM as his daughter or son.

And that is what is so AMAZING about God's grace:

It's illogical; it's undeserved; it is unnecessary…

But it is also utterly wonderful.

And if you want it, it is yours to keep for ever. God stands ready to embrace you in his loving arms—all you have to do is to turn towards him and take that first step on your journey home.

So let's celebrate God's love and acceptance as we sing "Amazing grace! How sweet the sound that saved a wretch like me! I once was lost but now am found, was blind but now I see."

4. THE LORD'S MY SHEPHERD

The Lord's my Shepherd, I'll not want;
He makes me down to lie
In pastures green; He leadeth me
The quiet waters by.

My soul He doth restore again,
And me to walk doth make
Within the paths of righteousness,
E'en for His own name's sake.

Yea, though I walk in death's dark vale,
Yet will I fear no ill;
For Thou art with me, and Thy rod
And staff me comfort still.

My table Thou hast furnishèd
In presence of my foes;
My head Thou dost with oil anoint,
And my cup overflows.

Goodness and mercy all my life
Shall surely follow me,
And in God's house for evermore
My dwelling-place shall be.

Words: Francis Rous (after King David)
Music (Crimond): Jessie Seymour Irvine

71

About this hymn

- "The Lord's My Shepherd" is based on Psalm 23—a poem from the Bible written by Israel's King David.

- David started life as a shepherd boy. The psalm follows a year in the life of a shepherd and his sheep, drawing a comparison with how God cares for his people.

- The words for this version of the hymn were developed by a group of Scottish Protestants and first appeared in 1650. The tune "Crimond" was written by Jessie Seymour Irvine in 1872.

Exploring the Christian faith

Psalm 23 paints a picture of God as a loving, good Shepherd, who…

- cares for his sheep daily,

- travels every step of their lives with them, and

- will bring them safely to their eternal home.

"[God] tends his flock like a shepherd: he gathers the lambs in his arms and carries them close to his heart."

ISAIAH 40:11

Questions to consider

- Was there anything that particularly struck you from the psalm?

- Where do you feel you are at the moment: in green pastures, or the valley of the shadow, or somewhere else?

- What difference would it make if you knew that God was your Shepherd, leading you through?

- How do you feel about your life's journey going forward?

- Do you think you are able to trust God to the end of your journey?

Prayer

In the book of Romans, Paul says this: "I am convinced that neither death nor life, neither angels nor demons, neither the present nor the future, nor any powers, neither height nor depth, nor anything else in all creation, will be able to separate us from the love of God that is in Christ Jesus our Lord."

(Romans 8:38-39)

Heavenly Father,

Thank you that if I choose to follow, you will be my good Shepherd, and you will be by my side through the best times, but also through the darkest of valleys, when life feels too hard, and you promise you will never leave me.

Please draw me closer to you. Lead me, protect me, and care for me, comfort and sustain me. I trust you to lead me through the rest of my life and to be by my side, whatever happens, for now and for evermore.

In Jesus' name,

Amen

Script for Session 4
"The Lord's My Shepherd"

A few years ago, Chris the sheep hit the headlines when he was found in the Australian bush not far from Canberra. Chris had been on the run for five years and, without anyone to shear him, had grown the heaviest fleece ever recorded, weighing in at 91lbs and over 17 inches long. It took five people to shear him, and although it could have made 30 jumpers, the fleece has instead taken pride of place in the National Museum of Australia!

The story of Chris reminds us that sheep really don't do very well in the wild; they need a shepherd to look after them. And in many ways so do we, which is why the Bible often uses the picture of a shepherd with his sheep to describe how God looks after his people. And perhaps the most famous example of that is Psalm 23, which this wonderful hymn is based on.

If you were with us when we sang "Amazing Grace", you may remember that we talked about how God lavishes us with his grace and how he longs to restore each one of us to a full and loving relationship with him.

And I hope and pray that all of us either have or will experience the reality of God's love, grace and forgiveness in our lives.

However, if we are honest, there are times in all our lives when we may not feel very "lavished"—when love, hope and grace feel a long way away.

For every one of us, there will be times in our journey through life when things are not so easy, when we may feel overwhelmed by difficulties or pain, and ever more so as we get older.

Failing health, loneliness, the death of friends and loved ones, the fear of our own death and future—these are very real challenges that we will all face at some point.

And for 3,000 years, in such times of struggle, people have turned to Psalm 23 for comfort, guidance and support.

The hymn we have just sung is one of many versions of this psalm set to music and is probably the best known. This version was actually put together over a period of 75 years by a group of Scottish Protestant thinkers and first appeared in 1650.

But of course, the psalm it is based on is much older, and that was written by King David, who was ruler of the ancient kingdom of Israel about 3,000 years ago.

David was the greatest king Israel ever had; he was powerful, victorious in battle and loved by his people. He was the 25 x great grandfather of Joseph, the adoptive father of Jesus, and, as well as being king, was also a significant spiritual leader who wrote a large number of poems and songs that are now part of the Bible.

He's appeared in paintings by Rembrandt and Caravaggio, as well as Michelangelo's famous statue of him in Florence.

But David wasn't always the sophisticated, handsome, psalm-writing king that he is depicted as in art.

He started life as a shepherd boy and in his early years would have spent much of his time away from home, living and travelling with his father's sheep.

And in this psalm, David draws on all this experience as he follows the journey through a year in the life of a shepherd and his sheep.

Psalm 23 starts at the home ranch, with the sheep relaxed in green pastures, grazing beside still waters. Here every need is met and the sheep are safe and well fed.

But as the summer heat comes, the grass will wither and the streams dry out, and so the shepherd must lead his sheep up into the mountains, where it is cooler and the grass is more succulent.

The journey there, through the dark valleys up the mountainsides, can be hazardous, with wolves, bears and lions to fend off—but when the sheep finally arrive at the high plateaus or tablelands as they are called, they will find the shepherd has already prepared the grass for them, and it will sustain them through the long, hot summer, while the shepherd will continue to protect them from predators with his rod and staff.

Then, once summer turns to autumn, the shepherd will lead his sheep back home for the winter months and back to safety.

It's a wonderful picture of love and care, and I think it tells us three things about our relationship with God, our good shepherd, if we choose to follow him.

Firstly, it tells us that the good shepherd cares for and tends his sheep every day.

Secondly, that he travels every step of the journey of their lives with them.

And finally, the good shepherd leads his sheep back to his home, where they are safe and looked after for ever.

So first: the good shepherd cares for and tends his sheep. The book of Isaiah says: "[God] tends his flock like a shepherd: he gathers the lambs in his arms and carries them close to his heart".

This is exactly the picture of daily love and care that David sees as he writes this psalm.

God is his Shepherd, and God is our Shepherd. He created us and redeemed us. He loves us as his own, just like the shepherd owns and cares for his sheep.

But just as God is our Shepherd, so we are like sheep and often in need of some shepherding!

Of all domesticated animals, sheep are the least able to look after themselves. They have no defence against predators; they cannot find their own food; they are susceptible to endless bugs and infections. As we saw with Chris, they can't even shed their own wool without the help of their shepherd.

Like us, they can also make some very poor decisions.

It is not that uncommon, for example, for a slightly overweight sheep to find a nice comfy hollow to lie in. But as it snuggles down, its centre of gravity can move, and suddenly it has rolled over, and none of its feet are touching the ground.

It's then stuck.

Shepherds refer to this as the sheep being cast: stuck on its back, legs waving in the air and unable to get up—not too dissimilar to how I feel when trying to get out of bed in the morning!

But, whilst this may be funny to us, it can be rather serious for the sheep: without getting too biological, gases begin to build up in its stomach, the blood supply is cut off from its legs and it rapidly gets weaker and weaker. If left alone, it will die.

But if a shepherd finds a cast-down

sheep, he can't just put it upright and walk away. He must turn it gently, rubbing its legs to bring the blood supply back and rubbing its stomach to let the gases go down, and then he still needs to support it until it is steady enough to walk by itself.

I think this is a wonderful picture of how God, our Shepherd, cares for us.

Like sheep, we will often look for the comfy hollow to settle in, choosing the easy life rather than following the shepherd.

We can get distracted and lost down the cul-de-sacs of life; but God is our wonderful Shepherd, who daily comes and picks us up, puts us gently on our feet and returns us to his flock.

As the psalm says, he restores our soul.

Secondly, a good shepherd journeys with his sheep. We all know that life is a journey, and there will be times when things are not easy, when we will find ourselves in a dark place, through no fault of our own, when we can't see where we are going and we are afraid.

And here the psalm promises us that God, our Shepherd, is by our side, journeying with us.

To get up into the mountains, the shepherd can't take the sheep along the ridges because the ground is too steep—instead he must take them up the narrow, deep and dark valleys.

Here the sheep can't see where they are going—it is dark; there are predators, so they have no choice but to trust the wisdom and protection of their shepherd.

In the same way, David encourages us to trust in our good Shepherd and allow God to lead us and walk alongside us as we pass through those dark times when we can't see where we are going or what may be coming up from behind.

But we should notice that David does not walk IN the valley of the shadow of death but THROUGH it. The sheep go THROUGH the valleys, either on their way to the fresh grass of the high plateaus or on their way back home.

Like them, we will never stay permanently in the valleys. God will lead us out—either to a better place here or to our ultimate home in heaven—but either way, he promises to always walk with us through the dark times.

The other thing you may notice when you look at the psalm and hymn is that they both start by referring to God in the third person: "The LORD is my Shepherd", "He makes me lie down", "He leads me", "He guides me"—but as soon as we have passed through the valleys, the psalm turns to second person: "You are with me", "Your rod … comfort[s] me", "You anoint my head".

God never promises to insulate us from the hard times in life, but he does promise to be with us through them, by his Spirit. And if we stick with him through these times, then our relationship with him will deepen and strengthen.

It is as we follow him that we get to know him, and as we get to know him, so we begin to trust him, and as we trust him, so we become less fearful as we pass through the dark valleys.

Finally, David promises that God will lead us home: "Surely your goodness and love will follow me all the days of my life, and I will dwell in the house of the LORD for ever".

Ultimately, our journey through life will end. Whatever green pastures or dark valleys we are travelling through will finish, and there God promises to be with us and to take us safely home.

In saving us on the cross, Jesus didn't just save us for a better life here and now but for an ongoing relationship with God after we have died. Christians believe that we have been created to live for ever and therefore created to spend that eternity with God.

But what will that look like? I don't know about you, but the thought of sitting on a cloud strumming a harp for ever doesn't fill me with joy.

So, it has to be better than that!

Well, what we do know is that it will be physical and not so dissimilar to what is around us now. The Bible talks about a new earth—one like this one but perfect. It will therefore be much the same as living on earth but also totally different, with no pain, no death, no tears.

The writer C.S. Lewis expresses it brilliantly. At the end of *The Last Battle*, his final book set in the land of Narnia, that world is drawn to an end, and as he looks forward to what happens next, C.S. Lewis says this:

"And for us this is the end of all the stories, and we can most truly say that

they all lived happily ever after. But for them it was only the beginning of the real story. All their life in this world and all their adventures in Narnia had only been the cover and the title page: now at last they were beginning Chapter One of the Great Story which no one on earth has read: which goes on for ever: in which every chapter is better than the one before."

As we head towards "Chapter One" of that great story, Psalm 23 tells us that we can know and trust God, our good Shepherd, to be there with us and to lead us safely to his home.

So, can I encourage you to put your life in his hands again and to trust his love?

If we let him, he has promised to protect us every step of the way, no matter what challenges and hardships we face, no matter how easy or how dark the valleys we travel through are. God, our good Shepherd, will be with us to the very end and for evermore.

5. AND CAN IT BE?

And can it be that I should gain
An int'rest in the Saviour's blood?
Died He for me, who caused His pain?
For me, who Him to death pursued?
Amazing love! How can it be
That Thou, my God, shouldst die for me?

He left His Father's throne above,
So free, so infinite His grace;
Emptied Himself of all but love,
And bled for Adam's helpless race:
'Tis mercy all, immense and free,
For, O my God, it found out me.

Long my imprisoned spirit lay
Fast bound in sin and nature's night;
Thine eye diffused a quick'ning ray,
I woke, the dungeon flamed with light;
My chains fell off, my heart was free,
I rose, went forth and followed Thee.

No condemnation now I dread;
Jesus, and all in Him, is mine!
Alive in Him, my living Head,
And clothed in righteousness divine,
Bold I approach th' eternal throne,
And claim the crown, through Christ my own.

Charles Wesley

About this hymn

- Charles Wesley was born in 1707 as the 18th of 19 children. He wrote over 6,500 hymns in his lifetime.

- As young men, Charles and his brother John were known for taking their religion very seriously. They and their friends were nicknamed the "holy club" or "Methodists".

- Everything changed for them in 1738 when they truly encountered God's grace for the first time. "And Can It Be?" was inspired by this experience.

Exploring the Christian faith

If we're trusting in Jesus, we can be confident to draw near to God as our Father because...

- Our relationship with God does not depend on us and what we do.

- Instead, it depends on Jesus and what he has already done for us through his death and resurrection.

"Since we have a great high priest who has ascended into heaven, Jesus the Son of God ... Let us then approach God's throne of grace with confidence, so that we may receive mercy and find grace to help us in our time of need."

HEBREWS 4:14, 16

Questions to consider

- Was there anything that particularly struck you from this session?

- Have you ever known someone (perhaps it's you) who has tried to earn God's acceptance through what they do? What are the problems with that approach?

- What's different about the Christian message ("the way of done", as the talk put it)?

- If a person believes that Jesus has done everything they need for them, what kind of life will they lead?

- How do you think it would feel to put your trust completely in what Jesus has done? Is that something you've done or would like to do—or are you still thinking about it?

Prayer

My Lord and my God,

Thank you that you made me, and you love me.

Thank you that your love and acceptance isn't based on my goodness but on the goodness of Jesus and his death on the cross.

I am so sorry for the times I have lived away from your ways, and I ask for your forgiveness.

I now turn to you and accept your amazing gift of forgiveness and eternal life.

I give my life to you and ask you to be my Lord.

Please fill me with your love today and help me to live for you by the power of your Holy Spirit.

Thank you.

Amen

Script for Session 5
"And Can It Be?"

Hello! We've reached the final session of our journey exploring the Christian faith through some of our most-loved hymns. We've come a long way!

You may remember that we started by singing "How Great Thou Art" and through that hymn explored how God was the powerful Creator of the trillions of stars that make up the universe.

We saw how his power and his "godliness" make him different from us—or "holy", as the Bible calls it—and that this means, whether we like it or not, that there is a large gap between us and God—a gap that by ourselves we can't close.

However, we also considered that this same big God loves us and wants to be in relationship with us—he wants to close that gap—and that he achieved this through the life and, in particular, the death of Jesus on the cross.

And that is what we explored when we sang the hymn "Rock of Ages".

This is probably the most personally challenging of all the hymns we have sung because it shows us that before God, we are completely helpless, totally lost and in need of rescuing.

But it also shows us that this is the point where God finds us and where we discover that, in his eyes, you and I are utterly priceless, of infinite value, and that God loves us so much that he paid the ultimate price, the highest possible price, to redeem us—to buy us back so we can become part of his family.

And that is what we discussed when we sang "Amazing Grace"—that the story of Jesus doesn't end with the cross; it goes on to his resurrection.

And through the story of the prodigal son, we saw how God lavishes us with love and grace—going far beyond just forgiving us, by restoring to us the right to be his sons and daughters in a close, loving relationship with him.

And then, last time we met, we sang "The Lord's My Shepherd" and reflected that this restoration, no matter how wonderful it is, doesn't insulate us from all the challenges of life.

But rather, if we choose to be in a relationship with God and allow him to be our Shepherd, he can and will be our Guide and Comforter on every step of our journey through life.

God's grace is not a one-off transaction but an ongoing relationship; God will be with us in the easy green meadows but also in the deep, dark valleys of life.

And so we come to today's hymn, which I must admit is one of my personal favourites, and it starts with a question: "And can it be that I should gain an interest in my Saviour's blood?"

And that may be where some of us are today. We probably wouldn't use the same 18th-century language, but we may well be wondering, "How can someone like me be of interest to someone like God?"

Well, the encouraging thing is that Charles Wesley, who wrote this hymn, took a long time to get his head around the answer to that question and to grasp just how GOOD the good news of the Christian message is.

But when he eventually did, it transformed his life and gave him so much confidence in God's love and acceptance that he could finish his hymn with the incredible statement, "Bold I approach the eternal throne".

Charles had discovered that God's love and forgiveness for him was so strong that he could walk straight up to God, with his head held high, confident that God loved him and accepted him.

But how did he get to this point? Well, I think we can find some of the answers through the story of his life.

Charles Wesley and his older brother, John, are best known as the founders of the Methodist church and the leaders of what is now known as the Great Awakening, a huge revival of Christianity in the mid 1700s.

John Wesley was the more famous as a preacher, but it was Charles who wrote the hymns. And boy, did he write hymns: over 6,500 of them—that's the equivalent of 2 ½ new hymns a week, every week for 50 years: week in, week out with no breaks and no holidays!

But his parents were also not lacking in energy. Charles was the 18th of 19 children produced by Susanna and Samuel Wesley. And rather than be totally exhausted by that feat, they still found time for Samuel to be a parish priest, writer and poet, and for Susanna to teach all of their children at home for six hours a day so proficiently that as a child Charles could reel off, by heart, long passages of the poet Virgil in the original Latin!

Frankly, I really don't know what I've been doing for most of my life to have achieved so little!

But this work ethic was then reflected in the way Charles and John went about their religion.

At university, Charles set up what became known as the Holy Club. It was a group of students who were almost fanatical in their pursuit of living a devout religious life.

They set aside time to pray during every single hour they were awake, and if that wasn't enough, they also met for a further three hours every day to focus entirely on prayer and Bible study, as well as visiting prisons and caring for the sick.

They were earnest and honourable but fell into the age-old mistake of thinking their behaviour could earn and improve their status before God.

They were so rigid that people mocked them for following such strict, unbending methods, and so soon they began to be called "Methodists"—a term which stuck with them for their rest of their lives.

However, Charles knew that for all his outward piety, he still felt dissatisfied internally.

For all his efforts, he hadn't managed to earn his way to a closer relationship with God. Something was missing.

But then, on 21 May 1738 in London, at the house of a man called John Bray, everything changed for Charles. He let go of all of his efforts and just let God into his life. Suddenly Charles understood, and then encountered, the grace of God and the love, forgiveness and joy that followed from relying not on the things he did for God but on what Jesus had done for him.

Three days later his brother John experienced the same, and the impact of this changed the whole of Britain. The Great Awakening had begun.

And if we want to know how Charles felt about this, then today's hymn tells it all. Written just after this experience, it shows how his black-and-white world of duty and obligation had been transformed into the technicolour of relationship and love, and that's why he could say, "I woke, the dungeon flamed with light; my chains fell off, my heart was free, I rose, went forth, and followed Thee".

So what about you and me? Can we say those words of freedom and delight with the same conviction as Charles? Which part of Charles' life do we follow?

Which path should we walk down?

Should we, like the younger Charles Wesley, choose the way of "do"—the route where we try to be religious enough to please God, following strict rules to try to DO enough to earn God's favour.

Or do we follow the Charles Wesley of today's hymn, and head down the way of "done". Here, we accept that we can't DO anything to earn God's love and acceptance because everything has already been DONE by Jesus.

You may remember that when we sang "Rock of Ages", we briefly reflected how Christianity is different from any other religion because it gives us no role in our salvation other than to say thank you.

But I think, if we are honest, even if we can agree with that in principle, in today's culture that can be hard for us to completely embrace. Many of us are so ingrained with a strong work ethic—we have to earn money, earn respect, earn the chance to retire—that we can be suspicious of something given for free, with no effort from ourselves and with no strings attached. And, like the early Charles Wesley, we then bring this thinking into our approach to God.

The sad fact is that if you ask most people, including many within the church itself, what Christianity is about, they will say it is about being good: going to church on Sundays, singing the right hymns, being kind to people, living a good life…

Or, if they are more cynical, they may say it is about being a goody-goody, a spoilsport—frowning on fun, judging others and arrogantly criticising everyone else's behaviour.

Both are so far from the truth because they place us, not Jesus, at the centre of our own salvation. They are at risk of turning our relationship with God into a sort of contract: he's done his bit in sending Jesus to die for us; now we just need to do our bit by being good if we are going to keep the prize.

But, as I hope we have seen over the last few weeks, the Christian faith is the exact opposite of that. It is not about what we can DO for God; it is all about what God has DONE for us.

Now, of course, that doesn't mean that how we behave doesn't matter. Jesus talked a lot about how we should behave, how to lead a good life, what standards we should aim for…

BUT the motivation for this is so different. God is not pushing us into a certain level of behaviour through fear or guilt—rather our behaviour is simply a response to the love and grace we have received, as he fills us with his Holy Spirit and helps us to change.

As is often the case, Shakespeare has a wonderful analogy. In the play *Anthony and Cleopatra*, Anthony describes his love for Cleopatra like this: "My heart was to thy rudder tied by th' strings".

For a Christian, the desire to live a good life is not about being pushed by fear but being pulled by love: as if our hearts were tied by string to God, so that wherever he leads, our heart follows.

And isn't this so much better? The way of grace says everything has already been done by Jesus on the cross; there is nothing you or I can do to make it any better.

It tells us there is nothing we can do to make God love us any more than he already does, but equally, there is nothing we can do to make him love us any less.

His love is perfect, complete, unending and undiminishing.

It cannot be weakened, and it cannot be lost.

And it is poured out on you and me.

The wonderful good news of Christianity is that all you and I need to do is to rely on Jesus… It is Jesus, not us, who has made us good enough. The Father has adopted us; we have become his children.

And that is why Charles Wesley could end his hymn so positively:

"No condemnation now I dread … [I'm] clothed in righteousness divine,

"Bold I approach th' eternal throne,

89

and claim the crown, through Christ my own."

Because of what Jesus has done, you and I do not need to be ashamed or nervous when we approach God, but rather we can approach God with confidence.

Not an arrogant confidence in ourselves and what we've done but confident in God and what he's done.

Confident that if we ask, he will lead us by the hand through the rest of our lives and beyond.

Confident that if we give him our life, it will be safe in those hands both now and for eternity.

SEASONAL SPECIALS

CHRISTMAS

HARK! THE HERALD ANGELS SING

Hark! The herald angels sing,
"Glory to the newborn King!
Peace on earth and mercy mild
God and sinners reconciled!"
Joyful, all ye nations rise;
Join the triumph of the skies;
With the angelic host proclaim:
"Christ is born in Bethlehem!"

*Hark! The herald angels sing,
"Glory to the newborn King!"*

Christ, by highest heav'n adored,
Christ, the everlasting Lord!
Late in time behold Him come,
Offspring of the Virgin's womb.
Veiled in flesh the Godhead see;
Hail the incarnate Deity,
Pleased as man with man to dwell.
Jesus, our Emmanuel.

*Hark! The herald angels sing,
"Glory to the newborn King!"*

Hail the heav'n-born Prince
                      of Peace!
Hail the Sun of Righteousness!
Light and life to all He brings,
Ris'n with healing in His wings.
Mild He lays His glory by,
Born that man no more may die,
Born to raise the sons of earth,
Born to give them second birth.

*Hark! The herald angels sing,
"Glory to the newborn King!"*

Charles Wesley

About this hymn

- It was written by Charles Wesley—author of over 6,500 hymns, including "And Can It Be?"

- This carol began life in 1739. Charles' original tune was much more sombre, and its first line was "Hark how all the welkin rings, 'glory to the King of kings'".

- The words went through many revisions after Charles' death. In 1856, William Cummings adapted the words to fit a new cantata Felix Mendelssohn had written to commemorate the 400th anniversary of the printing press.

Exploring the Christian faith

The story of Christmas is the story of God's Son, Jesus, coming into our world on a rescue mission. This Christmas he offers us…

- The gift of comfort—knowing that Jesus is with us in the midst of our sadness and struggle.

- The gift of hope—as we trust in Jesus' life, death and resurrection for forgiveness, and look forward to a wonderful future with God.

"For God so loved the world that he gave his one and only Son, that whoever believes in him shall not perish but have eternal life. For God did not send his Son into the world to condemn the world, but to save the world through him."

JOHN 3:16-17

Questions to consider

- Did anything from the talk strike you in particular?

- How are you feeling about the Christmas season and the end of another year? In what ways do you need comfort and hope?

- What does it tell us about God that he would come into our world—not as a VIP but as a poor and helpless baby?

- What would it look like for you to begin to unwrap Jesus' two gifts of comfort and hope? Or are there questions that you need to have answered first?

Prayer

Dear Lord,

Thank you so much for Christmas—that 2,000 years ago you sent your son, Jesus, to be born in a stable so he could rescue the world… and also rescue me.

I ask that you help me to know your comfort and your hope this Christmas. Thank you that these gifts are ready and waiting for me—I don't need to do anything extra or special to earn them; I just need to accept them.

Please watch over me, my family and friends today and over the coming weeks, and help each of us to know your comforting presence by our side and your bright hope for a future spent with you.

In Jesus' name, we pray.

Amen

Script for Christmas Session "Hark! The Herald Angels Sing"

Happy Christmas! I am one of those people who loves everything about Christmas and the Christmas season—from the time I spend with family and friends to the lovely food and, of course, giving (but mainly receiving!) presents. But I also love the story of the nativity and those little nativity scenes that some of us may have in our homes or may see in local churches—you know, the ones with a crib and lots of animals.

And when I look at those scenes, it's often the camels, lurking at the back, that catch my eye. They seem to me to be one of the more interesting creatures in the Christmas story. Traditionally, they are what the wise men rode on to find Jesus. And when I think about them, they remind me that Jesus was born into a very different world from the one we live in now.

But they are also rather odd creatures if you think about—all funny humps, bad tempers and really tricky to ride; they just don't seem to be very well designed. As one famous designer once said, "A camel is a horse designed by a committee."

And I know the feeling: to use another well-known phrase, too many cooks spoil the broth—so often, when lots of people get involved with designing something, what results can be a bit of a mess.

But thankfully that cannot be said about "Hark! The Herald Angels Sing". It is probably my favourite Christmas carol, but the version we know and love today has been changed and updated by a whole range of people over the years.

It began life way back in 1739 when Charles Wesley first wrote what he called his "Hymn for Christmas Day". But that started with the less-than-catchy line "Hark how all the welkin rings 'Glory to the King of kings'". And "welkin", in case you're wondering, is an old English word for the sky.

Charles and his older brother, John Wesley, were the founders of the Methodist movement and leaders of what is now known as the Great Awakening, a huge revival of Christianity in the 1700s.

And whilst John did most of the

preaching, it was Charles who wrote the songs that became the soundtrack to this movement.

In total he wrote around 6,500 hymns, many of which we still sing today, including "And Can It Be", "O for a Thousand Tongues to Sing" and "Love Divine, All Loves Excelling".

And although things like copyright didn't exist in those days, Charles was very resistant to any changes to his lyrics, or to music that he felt didn't fit his words.

And in the case of his "Hymn for Christmas Day", not only did he want the "welkin rings" kept in; he insisted that it be set to slow, solemn music, to help people better appreciate the true depth of God's amazing love shown at Christmas.

Sadly for him, but happily for us, neither of his wishes were fulfilled.

Over the next few years the lyrics were edited and developed by numerous different people to be much closer to what we know today.

But there was still no settled music to fit the carol. It was only in 1856, nearly 120 years after Wesley first wrote it, that William Cummings, a renowned tenor and professor at the Royal Academy in England, noticed how well the updated version of Wesley's carol could fit a cantata that Felix Mendelssohn had recently composed to commemorate the 400th anniversary of the printing press.

To make it fit perfectly, Cummings had to make even more changes to both the words and to the music, but when [it was] complete, he was able to finally publish the version of "Hark! The Herald Angels Sing" which we know and love today, and which remains one of most lyrically thoughtful and musically uplifting of all our Christmas carols.

But whilst the story of the writing of this carol may be a bit messy, the story the carol points us to certainly isn't. The events of the first Christmas were not the work of a bumbling committee but the story of just one man, Jesus, sent by God to transform our world.

John 3:16, possibly the most famous verse in the Bible, says, "For God so loved the world that he gave his one and only Son, that whoever believes in him shall not perish but have eternal life".

And it goes on: "For God did not

send his Son into the world to condemn the world, but to save the world through him".

And that is the true story of Christmas—not the story of God forming a committee to solve our problems but of God getting deeply and personally involved in our messy world, in order to restore our relationship with him.

It is the story of how God's love for you and for me led him to send his Son, Jesus, on the most amazing rescue mission.

And that rescue mission started in a stable in Bethlehem 2,000 years ago.

And at the heart of the Christmas story, and at the centre of this carol, are two things: comfort and hope.

COMFORT: that Jesus is here with us now, right by our side this Christmas, longing to shower us with his love and support us with his presence.

And secondly, HOPE: you see, the story of Jesus doesn't end with a baby in the manger because that baby grew up and went on to complete his rescue mission to save the world, and that offers us a bright hope for a better tomorrow.

And comfort and hope are things that all of us need.

Christmas is often a time for reflection; a chance to look back on the year that is ending and to consider all that has happened during that time.

And as we do that, I'm sure there will be some of us who can look back and be thankful for a lovely year filled with good times and happy memories. We may well be looking forward to a lovely Christmas with our family and friends and a chance to overindulge in food, drink and presents.

But for many others of us, I suspect the year will not have been so easy.

We may be grieving for lost family or friends, we may have been ill ourselves, we might find ourselves alone and lonely…

We may be struggling with financial insecurity or crippling anxiety.

And so, understandably, as we look towards Christmas, we may feel there is very little to celebrate—very little to look forward to.

But whichever type of year we have had and whatever type of Christmas we are facing, we can know that

God will be right beside us as we go through it, sharing in our joys but also sharing in our troubles.

The true story of Christmas is that just over 2,000 years ago, a baby called Jesus was born in an outbuilding in a small Middle-Eastern village, in a remote, unimportant outpost of the Roman Empire.

But the Bible tells us that this tiny, fragile, helpless baby was also the image of the invisible God: that all things—from the stars to the earth to you and I—were created through him and for him, and that ALL the fullness of God was contained within him.

As Wesley so beautifully puts in this carol, God is "pleased as man with man to dwell, Jesus [is] our Emmanuel".

The word Emmanuel means, "God with us".

And isn't that just so wonderful? We don't have a remote, distant God who doesn't know or care about our daily lives.

We have a God who chose, in love, to lower himself—to experience the limitations of human form—so that you and I can know that

he understands us and meets us in whatever place we find ourselves this Christmas.

Because the other thing is Jesus didn't come as a prince or a VIP. The nativity story reminds us that he was born into dirt and poverty, wrapped in cloths and placed in an animal feeding trough.

He went on to become a refugee, and he grew up in an occupied nation where he would have experienced hunger and persecution.

The path God chose for himself when he came to earth was to be poor, to struggle, to face hardship, fear and loss…

And that is why we can be confident that he understands when we struggle, when we are fearful and anxious and when we grieve.

He is not distant and above us at those times but right beside us, holding our hands, feeling our pain and comforting us in his love.

But Jesus does even more than this because the nativity is not the end of the story. The story of Christmas would have little meaning if it did not go on to the story of Easter. Jesus not only offers to comfort us this

Christmas; he offers a real, tangible hope for the future.

That baby in the manger grew up to become the man Jesus and—through his life, death and resurrection—can give us a real hope for the future, totally restoring our position with God, bringing forgiveness, reconciliation and an ongoing and deep love-filled relationship. He has offered us a completely new clean start.

The passage from John 3:16 that I referred to earlier is part of a conversation between Jesus and a Jewish religious leader called Nicodemus.

That conversation begins with Jesus saying that to follow God, we need to be born again.

It is an image Jesus uses to show what God does in our lives when we accept his gift of forgiveness—from that moment, we're effectively starting again, given new lives transformed by God.

That's what it means to be "born again". And this is at the heart of why Jesus was born in Bethlehem, as Charles Wesley says:

"Mild He lays His glory by,

Born that man no more may die,
Born to raise the sons of earth,
Born to give them second birth."

As Jesus told Nicodemus, and as he tells each of us today, if we accept his gift of forgiveness, we will have eternal life; we can live in a restored relationship with God.

"Peace on earth and mercy mild, God and sinners reconciled."

The true, deep, real peace that Jesus offers to each of us this Christmas is the peace and reconciliation that is available between us and God.

The peace on earth that we sing about is not primarily about peace between humankind.

Of course, that is hugely important, and we should do all we can to live in peace with others, but there will never be deep and lasting peace between mankind if there is not deep and lasting peace between each of us and God.

And all we have to do to find this is accept the gift that Jesus is offering us.

And so, this Christmas, whatever kind of Christmas you are facing—whether it is one filled with love and joy or one of loneliness, fear or grief, or maybe a mixture of both—can I encourage you to imagine two extra presents for you to unwrap—gifts to you personally from Jesus, that baby in the manger?

The first is his gift of comfort: his presence right beside you in your joy and celebration or in your troubles and fears, sharing your happiness but also sharing your pain.

And the second present is his promise of a hope for the future: an everlasting peace and joy, reconciled to him through what Jesus has done.

My prayer for each one of us this Christmas is that we will unwrap these two presents, accept them for the gift that they are and, through them, find the comfort, joy, peace and hope that they bring.

And of course, that each of us will have a genuinely Happy Christmas.

EASTER

THINE BE THE GLORY

Thine be the glory, risen, conqu'ring Son;
Endless is the victory Thou o'er death hast won;
Angels in bright raiment rolled the stone away,
Kept the folded grave-clothes where Thy body lay.

Thine be the glory, risen, conquering Son;
Endless is the victory Thou o'er death hast won.

Lo! Jesus meets us, risen from the tomb;
Lovingly He greets us, scatters fear and gloom;
Let the church with gladness, hymns of triumph sing,
For her Lord now liveth: death hath lost its sting.

Thine be the glory, risen, conquering Son;
Endless is the victory Thou o'er death hast won.

No more we doubt Thee, glorious Prince of life;
Life is naught without Thee: aid us in our strife;
Make us more than conquerors, through Thy deathless love;
Bring us safe through Jordan to Thy home above.

Thine be the glory, risen, conquering Son;
Endless is the victory Thou o'er death hast won.

Edmond Budry

About this hymn

- "Thine Be the Glory" was written by the Swiss hymn-writer Edmond Budry in 1884.

- Edmond was born in Vevey—the home of milk chocolate—and later became a pastor there.

- He set the hymn to a tune composed by George Handel some 140 years previously.

- It was translated from French into English in 1923.

Exploring the Christian faith

- The claim that Jesus rose from the dead is central to the Christian message. It shows that God can be trusted, forgiveness is possible, death is defeated and heaven is attainable.

- The risen Jesus patiently and lovingly met his followers in their fear and doubt, and brought them to a place of joy and confidence—and he offers to do the same for us.

"When the disciples were together, with the doors locked for fear of the Jewish leaders, Jesus came and stood among them and said, 'Peace be with you!' After he said this, he showed them his hands and side. The disciples were overjoyed when they saw the Lord."

JOHN 20:19-20

Questions to consider

- Was there anything in the talk that particularly struck you?

- Which characters in the Easter story did you most identify with, and why?

- Why did Jesus' resurrection so transform his first followers? Why is it still significant for Christians today?

- How would you describe what Jesus is like, based on what you've heard today?

- As you consider Christianity, what questions, doubts or fears do you have? Would you be willing to bring them to Jesus and let him meet you in them?

Prayer

Dear Lord,

Thank you that no matter where I am today, you are able to find me, to come by my side and to call me by my name. Thank you that you are not put off by my doubts, uncertainty, or fears, but that because of Jesus, you will always be ready to welcome me, just as I am.

Help me now to put my trust in you, knowing that being held in your arms is the safest place to be.

I ask, dear Lord, that over the coming days, you would help me draw close to you, listen to your voice and come to know just how much you love me.

In the name of Jesus, I pray.

Amen

Script for Easter Session "Thine Be the Glory"

Imagine the scene 2,000 years ago on the first Easter Sunday morning—Jesus' closest friends have spent the weekend in shock and in hiding. Jesus—the man they had left everything behind to follow for the last three years, the man in whom they had placed their trust and hope for a better future, the man whom they all loved more than anyone else—has gone.

Just two days earlier, they had watched his execution, as the Roman soldiers nailed Jesus to a wooden cross to die. And with his death, their hopes of a bright future had died too. The brave new world they thought they were creating had ended in failure, and they have spent these last two days in hiding, afraid for their very lives.

Suddenly there is a knock at the door. The disciples Peter and John open it to find Mary Magdalene, one of Jesus closest friends, standing there in tears. She has just been to visit Jesus' grave with some friends, only to find that the stone from the entrance has been moved. "They have taken the Lord out the tomb," she sobs, thinking the authorities have snatched the body,

"and we don't know where they've put him".

So the three of them grab their shoes and run to the tomb. John's the quickest and gets there first. He finds the tomb has been opened, but for some reason he holds back from going in.

Peter then arrives panting behind him, and being the strong character he is, he charges straight into the tomb to see for himself what has happened. And there, instead of finding Jesus' body, he finds the burial cloths that Jesus had been wrapped in, folded and left neatly in his place.

None of them can understand or explain what has happened, and although John seems to have some inkling, the others are just even more confused.

Certainly, neither Mary, Peter nor John at this point can respond with the sense of victory and joy with which we have just sung. But over the coming hours it all becomes clear: Jesus' body hasn't been stolen; he has risen—and the disciples' encounters with the resurrected Jesus will take each of them on a journey from a place of despair and grief to one of joy and hope for the future.

And this is the journey that Edmond Budry, who wrote this wonderful hymn, takes us on today. From the empty tomb with the rolled-away stone and folded grave clothes, through Jesus' appearance to the disciples in the locked room, where he "scatters" their "fear and gloom", to his promise, as our "glorious Prince of life", to "bring us safe through Jordan to [our] home above"—through the trials and challenges of life to an eternity safe by his side.

Edmond Budry was born in Vevey, Switzerland, in 1854. Vevey is a small, pretty town on the shores of Lake Geneva, but despite its modest size, it's been home to a host of famous authors, actors and artists over the years, from Charlie Chaplin to Graham Greene to David Bowie amongst many, many others. But in my opinion, the best thing about Vevey is that it was here that Henri Nestle helped to invent milk chocolate.

And what would Easter be without chocolate?

Unlike me though, Edmond was

not one to be swayed by such shallow things and instead moved to nearby Lausanne to study theology, becoming a free church pastor at the age of 27, and then returning a few years later to Vevey, where he remained a pastor for the next 35 years until he retired.

He also wrote and translated a number of hymns, but this is by far his most famous, which he wrote specifically to go with this wonderful rousing tune, composed by George Handel 140 years earlier.

Budry knew that the events of that first Easter Sunday morning are at the centre of the Christian faith—that the resurrection of Jesus was essential to making his faith meaningful. In fact, one of the writers of the Bible, the apostle Paul, wrote that "if Christ has not been raised, your faith is futile".

But equally, if Jesus really DID rise from the dead on that first Easter morning, then the implications are breathtaking, and everything the Bible says about Jesus is true: God can be trusted, forgiveness is possible, death is defeated and heaven is attainable.

And that is why the reality of

seeing and knowing a risen Jesus so transformed the lives of Mary and the disciples that Easter morning, and that's why we and Edmond Budry can sing so confidently:

"Thine be the glory, risen conquering Son; endless is the victory Thou o'er death hast won."

But as we just reflected, the journey that day didn't start so confidently. As Sunday dawned, everything appeared lost to the followers of Jesus. Grieving, fearful and defeated, they were not expecting a miracle and weren't ready for one.

But Jesus came gently and personally to each of them that day, meeting them at their point of need and turning their grief into joy, their fear into confidence and their defeat into victory.

Mary was the first to see Jesus. After she, Peter and John had seen the empty tomb, the two disciples returned to the city, but for some reason Mary lingered.

We don't know why she stayed; perhaps she wanted to be near the last place she had seen Jesus. Perhaps she just wanted to be alone to process all that happened. But we do know

that it was here that she became the first person in the world to meet the risen Jesus.

And yet, at first, she doesn't recognise him—she is, after all, hardly expecting to see him—so when he appears and asks her why she is crying, she assumes he is the gardener and wonders whether it is him who has moved the body.

But Jesus' response to this lack of recognition is both tender and beautiful—he simply and gently just speaks her name: "Mary".

She immediately recognises his voice, turns towards him and cries out, "Teacher".

It was not until Jesus spoke her name that Mary recognised him. But the moment he did, she knew it was him, perhaps because his voice was full of love for her.

Mary wasn't expecting to see Jesus that morning; she wasn't looking for someone to explain all the reasons why Jesus had to die and then rise from the dead. She was just grieving.

And that place of grief was where Jesus met her—not with fine words but with one word, "Mary", and that said everything that she needed to know because it said everything about how much he loved her.

They say that seeing is believing. But for Mary, and sometimes for us, seeing is not believing; being loved is.

But it was not just Mary who needed to encounter Jesus that day.

After she had recognised and hugged him, Jesus asked Mary to go and tell the disciples about everything that had happened—but, perhaps not surprisingly, they all, including Peter and John, seem to have struggled to believe her story.

Luke, in his Gospel, puts it wonderfully bluntly: Mary's words, he says, "seemed to them like nonsense". And as a result, we find them later that evening still fearful and still hiding behind locked doors.

And this is the place where Jesus meets them. John tells us he comes, stands among them and simply greets them: "Peace be with you".

He doesn't come to them in a flash of lightning. He doesn't tell them off for their lack of belief or for not understanding all his teaching over the previous three years. He just greets them and then, knowing how they are struggling to believe, shows them his wounded hands and side.

You see, whilst Mary needed to encounter Jesus with her heart, the disciples needed something more tangible—they needed the evidence of seeing Jesus close up, they needed him to show them his scars and they needed to hear his voice.

And so, just as Jesus had met the needs of Mary's heart, he now met the needs of the disciples' heads by coming to them just as they were, in their weakness and their fear.

And as they saw and experienced the risen Jesus, so they understood. Their fear and despair disintegrated and were replaced with astonishment and delight.

As we just sung: "Lovingly He greets us, scatters fear and gloom."

And what about you and me? I suspect that many of us may feel a bit like Mary, not quite sure of what we are looking for but knowing that there is something incomplete in our lives—a relational hole that perhaps only God can fill.

Maybe you are more like the disciples—full of doubts and wanting something more concrete than feelings to answer those doubts.

Or perhaps you identify more with the disciples' fears. Like them you feel shut away from the outside world. Maybe you feel lonely or possibly fearful.

Well, the wonderful story of Easter is that the risen Jesus comes to find you and me wherever we are, to stand before us, to speak our name, to show us his love, and to gently call us to believe and to follow.

Like the disciples, we don't need to leave the safety of our room, we don't need to resolve all our questions and fears, we don't need to go to church or follow a religious programme…

Jesus is not deterred by our questions or our doubts; he will meet us just where we are. And if we turn to him, we will find a Jesus who calls us by name, who shows, who explains, who welcomes and who forgives.

And if we place our trust in the risen Jesus [and] put our lives in his nail-scarred hands, he will, as Edmond Budry promises, scatter our fears and gloom. He will aid us in our strife and bring us safe through Jordan, through all the challenges and difficulties of life, to our home above. And then together we can all proclaim:

"Thine be the glory, risen conquering Son; endless is the victory Thou o'er death hast won."

MY SONG IS
LOVE UNKNOWN

My song is love unknown,
My Saviour's love to me,
Love to the loveless shown
That they might lovely be.
O, who am I,
That for my sake
My Lord should take
Frail flesh and die?

He came from his blest throne
Salvation to bestow;
But such disdain! So few
The longed-for Christ would
know!
But O, my Friend,
My Friend indeed,
Who at my need
His life did spend!

Sometimes they crowd His way
And His sweet praises sing,
Resounding all the day
Hosannas to their King.
Then "Crucify!"
Is all their breath,
And for His death
They thirst and cry.

They rise and needs will have
My dear Lord made away.
A murderer they save,
The Prince of life they slay.
Yet cheerful He
To suff'ring goes
That He His foes
From death might free.

In life, no house, no home
My Lord on earth might have;
In death, no friendly tomb,
But what a stranger gave.
What may I say?
Heav'n was His home,
But mine the tomb
Wherein He lay.

Here might I stay and sing;
No story so divine,
Never was love, dear King,
Never was grief like Thine.
This is my Friend,
In whose sweet praise
I all my days
Could gladly spend!

Samuel Crossman

About this hymn

- The words were written as a poem by Samuel Crossman, an English clergyman, in 1664.

- Following Samuel's death in 1683, the words were set to music and sung like a formal psalm for many years in Anglican churches.

- It wasn't until 1919 that it became the popular hymn we know and love today. The editors of England's *Public School Hymn Book* asked the composer John Ireland to come up with a new tune—which he's said to have done in just ten minutes on a scrap of paper!

Exploring the Christian faith

Christians believe that two things were going on during Jesus' final days:

- On a human level, Jesus was a real person who was brutally executed by the Roman authorities of his day.

- On a deeper level, God planned for this to happen. Jesus' death had a purpose—to show us God's love and to make us lovely in God's sight.

"God demonstrates his own love for us in this: while we were still sinners, Christ died for us."

ROMANS 5:8

Questions to consider

- Was there anything that particularly struck you from this session?

- We've heard that at the heart of the Christian faith is love. Is that what you would have said before this session? What word might you have chosen instead?

- Have you ever felt that God loves you? What makes you say that?

- How does Jesus' death on the cross show us God's love? What impact, if any, do you think Jesus' death has for you?

Prayer

Dear Lord,

Thank you so much for what Jesus did for us 2,000 years ago. Thank you for his life, for his sacrificial death and for his resurrection.

Thank you that through the awful hate and brutality of that last week, you showed just how much you love me.

Help me to receive and accept your love in my life and help me to allow you to change my life, so that I might be lovely in your eyes.

In Jesus' name, I pray.

Amen

Script for Any Time Session "My Song Is Love Unknown"

In 2013 two leading data scientists decided to find out, once and for all, who were the most significant figures in all of human history. And their approach to do this was nothing if not thorough—using complex computer programs, they reviewed and evaluated millions of comments and opinions written about famous people and from there produced a list that ranked over 200,000 people in terms of how significant they were in human history.

Some of these people had a relatively short period of influence. One of my favourite names on the list is Hugh "Iron Pants" Johnson; coming in at the relatively high position of 32,927, he was a leading player in President Roosevelt's New Deal, during the great depression, and was even named as *Time* magazine's Man of the Year in 1933, ahead of the president.

However, his significance quickly faded. Within a year, he had been sacked for his bad behaviour and never held a position of influence again.

In contrast to Iron Pants' brief moment of fame, the No. 1 person on the list is a man whose influence has lasted somewhat longer.

Jesus was born just over 2,000 years ago in a small village in a remote outpost of the Roman Empire, but to this day remains the most written-about and influential person who has ever existed, and is still loved, worshipped and followed by millions of people around the world.

The stories of Jesus' life are some of the best-known stories in all of history: his birth in a stable, the visits of the shepherds and the three kings, him turning water into wine and his feeding of the 5,000.

These stories have been shared and discussed by billions of people throughout history and have been the inspiration for endless books, films and television programmes.

But for Christians, the most important stories of all are those that centre around the last week of Jesus' life—from his triumphant arrival in Jerusalem on a donkey, through the Last Supper, his betrayal by a kiss from Judas, and on to his death on a cross and resurrection three days later.

And it is this final week that is captured so beautifully in the hymn we just sang. It reminds us of Jesus' arrival in Jerusalem, riding a donkey on the day we now call Palm Sunday. On that day, thousands came out to cheer him, shouting "Hosanna" and laying their cloaks and palm leaves on the ground for him to ride over.

But the hymn also reminds us that things quickly began to change: that just a few days later, those very same crowds rejected him. Rather than crying out "Hosanna", they now shouted "Crucify" and chose to save a murderer called Barabbas instead of Jesus. And that as a result, the following day, Jesus was nailed to a cross and died.

It was a distressing, violent and ugly end to Jesus' life...

And yet...

And yet...

Despite all that was happening physically, Christians believe that something beautiful—something filled with perfect love, something giving perfect hope—was also happening.

That through his cruel and painful death and through his resurrection three days later, Jesus turned the whole history of the world around, and can turn the whole direction of your life and mine around. And that is all because, Christians believe, these events were not driven or determined by the crowds or the authorities but were in fact driven by Jesus' love for you and for me.

As this hymn so beautifully puts it— "My Saviour's love to me, love to the loveless shown that they might lovely be."

And that is the reason why, 2,000 years later, Christians still see the death and the resurrection of Jesus as the most significant and important events in all of history. And these are what Samuel Crossman celebrates in this hymn, written over 350 years ago.

In it, he walks us through that final week of Jesus' life and to me seems to pull out two themes.

Through the middle of the hymn, he focuses on the injustice and cruelty of Jesus' treatment at the hands of the crowds and the authorities.

But he sandwiches that at the beginning and the end of the hymn by reminding us that this is not really a story about the physical trials and tribulations of that week but is in fact a song about the incredible love of God for you and me.

And these two themes seem to reflect something of Samuel's personal experience when he wrote this hymn in 1664.

He had been ordained a minister just four years earlier in 1660, right at the end of England's short period as a republic under Puritan rule. Samuel's sympathies were initially with the Puritans, and therefore when the monarchy returned and Charles II became king, he quickly fell out of favour with the new authorities and soon lost his job and income as a minister, as well as many of his friends.

In just a few short years, Samuel had gone from being supported and encouraged by the religious authorities to being rejected and thrown out by them. And it is perhaps this experience which led him to write the middle verses of this hymn which focus so much on the human rejection and treatment of Jesus in that final week.

However, in spite of all this, Samuel remained confident in the fact that God hadn't changed direction and God hadn't rejected him. No matter how loveless he felt, Samuel knew God still loved him and that is why, I think, he was able to express that love so beautifully when he wrote these words as a poem in the middle of his struggles with the church.

Happily for Samuel, his story ended well. A few years later he reconciled himself with the church authorities, returned to his ministry and was eventually appointed Dean of Bristol Cathedral.

Following his death in 1683, his poem "My Song Is Love Unknown" was set to music and sung like a formal psalm for many years as part of the canon of hymns within the Anglican church.

But it took another 250 years for it to become the popular hymn that we know and love today. In 1919, just after the end of First World War, the editors of England's *Public School Hymn Book* decided to revive the hymn and asked John Ireland, one of the leading composers of the day, to come up with a new tune...

And the story goes that Ireland was so inspired by the words that he wrote the entire music for the hymn in just ten minutes on a scrap of paper—

and it has remained unchanged for the hundred years since.

However, I think there is another reason why this hymn remains so popular, and that is the beautiful balance Samuel Crossman has created between the human drama of those events and the wonder of God's love that underpins them.

You see, on the human level, there is no doubt that Jesus existed. There really was a man named Jesus, who lived 2,000 years ago and who gathered around him a group of followers who were mistrusted by the local authorities. And this man was then arrested and tried by them, and executed by the Roman rulers in a horribly brutal way.

The evidence that this is all historical fact is overwhelming. The question is therefore not whether the story is true but whether that is all there is to the story—because Christians through the ages have believed that there was something else going on.

That in this story of brutality, there is in fact beauty.

That in this story of anger and hate, there is in fact love.

And that in this story of a physical death, there is in fact a story of spiritual birth.

Christians believe that the real story is that Jesus chose to die on a cross as the clearest way for us to see and experience just how much God loves us. That this is not just a physical story of a man from 2,000 years ago but a spiritual story of God's love that remains relevant today...

As Samuel Crossman puts it, there is "no story so divine, never was love, dear King … like Thine".

But if you are like me, or Samuel Crossman, you may well be asking, "Why?" Why would Jesus choose to die on a cross?

"Who am I," Samuel Crossman asks, "that for my sake my Lord should take frail flesh and die?"

If you visit London, you will find that above the door of the Protestant Westminster Abbey, there is a statue of a Catholic priest called Father Maximilian Kolbe.

At the beginning of the Second World War, Father Maximilian lived and worked at a monastery in central Poland. Following the German invasion, he was initially able to help shelter Jewish refugees but was soon arrested and, on 28th May 1941, sent to the concentration camp at Auschwitz.

After he had been there two months, another prisoner somehow managed to escape, and to punish those who remained, the camp commandant declared that ten prisoners must die by being starved to death.

The guards lined up all of the prisoners and then selected ten at random. But as they were being taken away to die, one of them, Franciszek Gajowniczek, cried out, "My wife, my children!"

As soon as he heard this, Father Maximilian, who had not been selected as one of the ten, stepped forward and said, "I am a Catholic priest, and I wish to die for that man". So Father Maximilian was taken in his place, and two weeks later, having not yet died of starvation, was killed by a lethal injection.

41 years on, 150,000 people attended a ceremony in St Peter's Square, Rome, to remember what Father Maximilian had done—and there amongst them were Francis and his wife.

Father Maximilian's death is a wonderful example of sacrificial love in action—how in the midst of horror, love can shine a bright light and how one man can substitute himself for another.

But Father Maximilian himself would be the first to acknowledge that even his death and his act of sacrificial love—no matter how generous and noble—were still just a small imitation of what Jesus achieved on the cross.

Because Christians believe that Jesus did not die for one man and his family but for all humankind, and that he did this because he loves you and me so much that he wants to save us, to restore us to a loving relationship with God.

But Jesus' sacrifice goes even further, because he doesn't just save our lives; he gives us the power to transform our lives. His love for us has a purpose, and that purpose is to help us become more like him—as Samuel Crossman puts it "that [we] might lovely be".

What Samuel Crossman knew, and what billions of Christians have known and experienced throughout history, is that at the centre of those events in Jerusalem 2,000 years ago, and at the centre of the Christian faith... is love:

God's love for us and, as we experience that, our growing love for him.

Despite what many people may think, Christianity at its core is not really about going to church; it's not really about reading and understanding the Bible; it's not even really about being good.

Those things are all important, but they are not the start or the finishing point. That is, and always will be, love: God's perfect, unending, unconditional, sacrificial love for you and for me.

And no matter how loveless or un-lovely we may feel, the wonderful story of those final days of Jesus' life is that he still loves you and me, and that if we choose to accept that love, he will come beside us, turn us around and make us lovely for evermore in his eyes.

And that is why our song is love unknown, our Saviour's love to us, love to the loveless shown that we might lovely be.

ACKNOWLEDGEMENTS

We would love to thank our children, Bel and Toby, and Pippa's parents, Tisha and David, for their ongoing love, support, encouragement and prayers, with a special mention to Pippa's mother, Tisha. We know that her hours of daily prayer over the years for *Hymns We Love* and Pippa's work have not been wasted. She is an inspiration to us, and she has helped Pippa realise just how vital prayer is. Pippa will be forever grateful.

A huge thank you to all those at Holy Trinity Claygate and all in the various teams Pippa is involved with at church for their encouragement, feedback and support for *Hymns We Love* over the recent years.

Pippa will be forever grateful for the wisdom of Holy Trinity Claygate's Terms of Reference Group, and for the small team consisting of Denise, Ruth, Lorraine and Jackie, who have provided such support and skill in the areas that Pippa is not good at!

We would both like to single out Denise Pavey here: her support, insight and experience have been invaluable. There are no words really. We are so thankful to God for the provision of the wonderful D—she has been the most incredible answer to prayer, and Pippa especially is aware that we would not be where we are today without her.

Steve would like to thank Rev'd Canon Chris Russell for his wisdom, guidance and input on Steve's first drafts of the *Hymns We Love* scripts. Chris is an inspiration to us both, and we have learnt so much from him and darling Belinda.

We would both love to thank and acknowledge all at The Good Book Company, our fantastic Publishers, especially Rachel Jones, our ever patient and wise editor, and Carl Laferton and James Burstow for catching the vision for *Hymns We Love* and for making it happen! We'd also very much like to reference Rico Tice here for his encouragement to get *Hymns We Love* published, and for his recommendation to work with The Good Book Company!

We'd like to thank Fruitmedia for being the most brilliant media team. We never realised filming could be so much fun! Their creativity and imagination, and their ability to transform our dream of *Hymns We Love* into a sparkling reality, have been such an inspiration to us.

We would love to thank the team (past and present) at Faith in Later Life for their support and encouragement of *Hymns We Love* and for their ongoing promotion of this. It's been a joy to work alongside such a wonderful group of like-minded people who share our passion for evangelism with those in later life.

A huge thank you to John Hatton and the extraordinary choir at Holy Trinity Brompton for so effortlessly producing the most beautiful renditions of each of the hymns. Their willingness to serve in this way has been truly humbling to us, and we are forever grateful.

Thank you also to St Mary's Church, Washington, and All Saints Church, Buncton, West Sussex, for providing the most perfect backdrop setting for the filming of the videos, and especially to John Yeo, churchwarden, for his help with this and for his interview and singing too!

Thanks and grateful appreciation to everyone who came along and sang as part of the choir and participated in the interviews. The films are just so much better because of these extraordinary individuals.

Pippa would love to thank her incredible grandparents, Omah and Grandpa. These two played such an important role in shaping Pippa's love, respect, and passion for older people generally; though they may not be with us now, they are forever etched in her mind and her heart.

And finally, our acknowledgements and greatest thanks go to our wonderful, incredible God, who has been and who continues to be our daily inspiration and first love. We are in awe of who he is, how much he loves us and what he has done for us—and we pray that hundreds of thousands of seniors all over the world will discover his great love for them through this resource, *Hymns We Love.*

thegoodbook
COMPANY

BIBLICAL | RELEVANT | ACCESSIBLE

At The Good Book Company, we are dedicated to helping Christians and local churches grow. We believe that God's growth process always starts with hearing clearly what he has said to us through his timeless word—the Bible.

Ever since we opened our doors in 1991, we have been striving to produce Bible-based resources that bring glory to God. We have grown to become an international provider of user-friendly resources to the Christian community, with believers of all backgrounds and denominations using our books, Bible studies, devotionals, evangelistic resources, and DVD-based courses.

We want to equip ordinary Christians to live for Christ day by day, and churches to grow in their knowledge of God, their love for one another, and the effectiveness of their outreach.

Call us for a discussion of your needs or visit one of our local websites for more information on the resources and services we provide.

Your friends at The Good Book Company

thegoodbook.com | thegoodbook.co.uk
thegoodbook.com.au | thegoodbook.co.nz
thegoodbook.co.in